Travels in Uruguay

John Hale Murray

D1457164

TENERIFFE AS SEEN TEN MILES OFF,

UPWARDS OF 12,000 FEET HIGH.

TRAVELS IN URUGUAY,

SOUTH AMERICA;

TOGETHER WITH

AN ACCOUNT OF THE PRESENT STATE OF

SHEEP-FARMING, AND EMIGRATION

TO THAT COUNTRY;

BY

THE REV. J. H. MURRAY, B.A.,

Late Chaplain in Colonia.

ILLUSTRATED WITH SKETCHES.

LONDON:

LONGMANS & CO., PATERNOSTER ROW.

E. STANFORD, CHARING CROSS.

1871.

PREFACE TO JOURNAL.

————•————

I SHALL be glad to find that the following attempt to make known the capabilities and beauty of the part of the South-American Continent in which I travelled may prove not only amusing but instructive to those who seek either a new field of investigation, or who wish to emigrate.

It is with the view of enlightening such persons as to the character of a part of the world of which so little is generally known, with the additional and more pleasing object to myself of recalling the most agreeable year of my life, that I have penned a recollection of my travels. And I shall be glad to know that any one who reads this book will put in practice and receive the same amount of instruction and enjoyment that I did, by taking a trip to those parts, so easily made; and, if in humble life, becoming a settler in a land of plenty and of increasing prosperity, so rapidly developing in every branch.

In the last portion of this book, I have referred to the operations of Sheep-farming as it is at present carried on in South America, and the business of settlers, so as to enable persons to judge of the advantage of entering on those pursuits and settling there.

In the former part, I note down my voyage out, with its scenes and usual routine of occurrences, and then the incidents that I personally met with in the solitary "gallops" that I constantly made through the open "camp," and crossing rivers, in a tract of country about eighty miles from north to south, by about seventy in width, during nearly a twelvemonth, besides a stay of some weeks in the cities of that country; and, I can truly say, I have a most happy recollection of the time I passed there.

CONTENTS.

———

CHAPTER I.

CHAPTER II.

CHAPTER III.

CHAPTER VI.

CHAPTER VII.

CHAPTER VIII.

CHAPTER IX.

CHAPTER X.

CHAPTER I.

I EMBARKED, on January 9th, 1868, in the *Tasmania,* one of the Royal Mail Company's steamers, from Southampton, in a frost so sharp that I could have skated from my hotel through the streets to the vessel. At whatever time of the year you quit England for South America, you will find that in a month you are placed in exactly an opposite season to that in which you were on leaving home. Therefore, by plunging from the inclement time of midwinter in England to the hottest midsummer season in Brazil, in a tropical zone, during the short interval of eighteen days, you will find it difficult to bear, and at first very trying.

The sea fortunately was calm, and we were told that the air would certainly be mild in two or three days' time, when, if the wind proved favourable, we should have run from 500 to 600 miles. If you can get across " the chops of the channel " and the Bay of Biscay without a west wind and gales, you may congratulate yourself with the almost certainty that all the rest of the voyage to Rio, for 4200 miles, will be a fine " yachting " voyage.

B

After the usual formalities at starting had been gone through, with a gentle bleeding of your pocket, in the shape of fees and dues, there was a general scrutiny of each other, among the passengers, so that each might form some estimate of the position, consequence, profession, and wealth, and, if possible, the peculiarities of his neighbour,—not however as yet proceeding to that skirmishing of personalities by which an Englishman is so readily distinguished from more polite foreigners. The passengers soon however began to sort, and to settle down in cliques, which seems to be the natural solution of English society, in such a predicament as this.

The vessel I was in was 372 feet long, and too narrow in beam for her length : consequently there was no pitching from stem to stern, but she was in a constant state of waddle, uncomfortable at times to those who are only accustomed to *terra firma*. The crockery was repeatedly sent flying; and sundry things tumbling down created unpleasant interludes throughout the night, that prevented sleep. And when the earliest dawn of light began, all the cocks on board, of which there must have been scores, seemed entitled to assert their privilege of proclaiming the day; and that with repeated salutations from one to another. "As the old cock crows, the young cock learns," was exemplified on this occasion. The senior seemed to commence his statement, and the juniors, according to age, reiterated it, which appeared to be, to them, a satisfaction, although they were crowded and heaped together, topsy-turvey, in the baskets. In spite of these disadvantages they found means of giving expression to their opinions; but it was anything but agreeable to the passengers. These unpleasant varieties prevailed throughout the voyage, though I could detect, as time wore on, that some of these birds had faded from the scene by appearing on the breakfast table.

The vessel itself was a noble one. It was not like going to sea, to be in a ship that could one way or other make up 300 berths. Its tonnage was 1700 register, or about 2500 actual; and capable, if both its sets of engines were used, of extending their power from 850 horse-power to more than double that amount, to meet a hurricane. In case of a cyclone this is a great advantage : for such a vessel, with its head put to the wind, and its greatest power on, would cut through water, wind, and waves alike. This had happened a year before to one of these fine vessels, in the Bay of Biscay, where she pierced through a tempest for twelve hours, with her steam power raised from 800 to 1500 horse-power.

We however met with no such unpleasantness, which is at all times exceptional. The ship was like a large modern hotel, with every comfort and luxury on board : plenty of ice, abundance of fresh distilled water, fruits, and flowers. There was none of the salt junk, hard biscuits, and stale water flavoured with rum, wherewith our old naval heroes, of the past generation, braved the battle and the breeze, and won their victories; but everything was so elegantly decorated and comfortable, that it would satisfy the most fastidious. Within four days we sighted land off Cape St. Vincent, and then kept along the coast of Portugal. The land seemed to be lofty, rugged, and with prominent rocks; and as we approached the entrance of the Tagus, we coasted along below Cintra, where stands the beautiful palace of the King of Portugal.

LISBON.

Some people extol the beauty of "the Panorama of the Tagus;" but I was greatly disappointed in its aspect. A large sand bank, or bar, in the centre of the entrance of the harbour, compels vessels to pass close to the side of it under an old Moorish tower, and fort. After this you proceed up the centre of the river, with the city rising from the water's edge up the hill, and ranging along on the left, for three miles. The ancient city was on the opposite side of the harbour, which was destroyed by the great earthquake of 1755, and was, with its pier thronged with people, engulphed in a vast depth. It is stated that in the place where the mole stood before the earthquake, there was afterwards found 100 fathoms deep of water; but certainly now there are only fifteen fathoms. No perceptible remains of that visitation are now to be seen. The hill, with a few houses on it, slopes down steeply to the water, leaving the imagination to supply the blank of what existed there where the old city, with its 60,000 inhabitants, once stood, and perished.

There are lofty houses of many storeys high in the city, the streets of which had a fishy and warehouse smell, and certainly were not in gay attire. Altogether I was not sorry to embark again; and, I must own, was greatly disappointed in the reported beauty of Lisbon and its Tagus.

We could feel a decided change in the weather,

though it was equally midwinter in Lisbon as with us in England; and we felt a mild genial tone in the air, such as orange trees rejoice to live in. Although we had gone only 900 miles, it was indispensable to replenish the ship's larder. Bullocks were hoisted on board by their horns, which did not seem to disturb the equilibrium of their minds; for they did not resist the operation, but took it as a matter of course, merely placing their feet on the deck as they were lowered upon it. Doubtless they trusted to the *mens conscia recti* of those that performed the operation upon them, as they showed a most philosophic indifference to the whole treatment.

We soon started for the great coaling station of St. Vincent, 1554 miles from Lisbon. After two or three days' further voyage, you get more sociable, and interested in your fellow voyagers. But at times a weariness comes over you, at the repeated sameness of scene and occupation, and from being out of sight of land.

We passed the Canary Islands and Madeira. The weather now began to be more than warm. The awning was spread over the deck every day, after breakfast; and you felt a soft summer air. The tops of the lofty and rocky islands rose above the horizon from vast depths, with a clearly defined and soft outline; and the beautiful sunset reminded you that you had taken leave of English fogs, and were approaching a tropical clime. On rising early the next morning we beheld

TENERIFFE,

ten miles off, rising perpendicularly upwards of 12,000 feet above the sea, equal to the highest points of the Pyrenees, and as high as many of the Alps.

We were fortunate enough to see it unshrouded in clouds, with its snow-clad peak shining like burnished silver in the morning sun, strongly in contrast with the brown-black of the hill below the peak, rent with black chasms, with the green vineyards extending in a line along its base, dotted with little towns and villages. The brown ridge of the mountain is 7000 feet high, the cone about 5000 feet. The former seemed, at ten miles off, to be split through its edge in various places; the peak itself rising probably two or three miles more inland from the summit of the brown and rugged hill. It presented a remarkable sight, so unlike anything else. Its top is seldom seen, as it is almost always enveloped in clouds.

In passing it, you do not realise its vast height. It is not until you go to a distance, that the top of the peak alone seems standing up in the vault of heaven, apparently detached from the rest of the mountains, and surrounded by the blue ether above and below.

We next reached St. Vincent Island, the coaling station for all the steamers going this way. It is a volcanic island, and remarkable for having no trees nor herbage, being nothing but cinders and sand: fruit and vegetables are imported from a neighbouring island. It is extensive, and has many pointed hills, some nearly 4000 feet high, but all barren, and the whole island is a desert. The people are blacks, speaking Portuguese, evidently with much negro blood in them. We walked a mile inland, and every place was in a state of desolation; big, black children running about in bare skin, and evidently not ashamed of appearing in nature's garb.

The offal and garbage lying about created an unpleasant smell. The only real business of the people seemed to be stowing away coals as they arrived from England, and loading steamers with them. If this were to cease, the island would doubtless return to its naturally desert state again. I observed that the steam power of the engine was applied for hauling many things, such as cattle and coals, on board, and for hauling up the anchor and sails, which must save much manual labour, compared to a mere sailing vessel. I was struck with the boat-loads of blacks, jabbering like a collection of monkeys—thin, scraggy fellows, in bathing costume, begging for a coin to be thrown into the water to them, when they would wait a while, and then dive after it, easily seeing and catching it at a great depth in the pellucid water. We received here the unpleasant news, from a steamer that arrived the day before, that cholera had broken out in Buenos Ayres, that 200 persons a day were dying of it, and that 120,000 persons had left the city for the camp to escape it.

We pursued our voyage, not expecting to touch land under 1620 miles. This perhaps was the most tedious part of the voyage. The passengers occupied themselves, some with chess, some of them in playing at "dumps," which consists in throwing flat round pieces of lead, enclosed in leather, on to a board that is divided into squares, and is marked with figures of different amounts. Those who make their dump rest on squares marked with the highest numbers, win, in a score of 1000. Every one had his seat assigned him at table. If an unfortunate and solitary Frenchman were placed near an

Englishman, in spite of his native politeness, he was sure to be joked, and annoyed with personal remarks; the inborn dislike of an Englishman to a Frenchman giving itself vent in such terms.

Two old sea captains, both of them English, had an argument which they resuscitated from day to day, as opportunity offered, about the great sea-serpent; the one considering it a veracity, the other a myth. I had forgotten the story, from its having occurred so long ago. Suffice it to say that, at the time it happened, an account of it, with a picture of the serpent, speeding along with its head raised out of the water, was thought worthy of being recorded and illustrated in the *Penny Magazine* of that period.

In the feud that repeatedly ensued on the question between these sea captains, I sat quiet, merely putting questions which were home thrusts to each side; appearing to be only a philosophic inquirer after truth, desiring to acquire facts, and to gain the fullest confirmation. The consequence was, that I became an involuntary judge on the occasion, both parties, like barristers, directing their arguments to me, as their common focus; each again and again returning to the charge; and that without requiring constant "refreshers," to stimulate their zeal. I, of course, was the most edified, if not highly amused, of the party.

The advocate for the truth of the vision of this great serpent thus stated his case. " As one of Her Majesty's ships was sailing in the South Atlantic an enormous serpent was seen to rise from the surface. It passed close to the vessel, with its head and neck some fifteen feet out of the water, at a rapid pace. Its supposed length was

about a quarter of a mile, "more or less," as Moore's Almanac
says about rain, on nearly every day of the month. It
was distinctly and closely seen by the officers and ship's
company of the vessel; and, what is more, the occurrence
was solemnly entered on the log of Her Majesty's said ship,
and was attested to by all the crew. And this was the
clencher to the argument "*pro.*" How was it possible or
likely that a captain of a man-of-war would enter this on
the log of his ship, if it was a fancy, and run the risk of
being hauled over the coals? A merchant vessel also
claimed to have seen it about the same time. Ancient
reports of the same sort have existed; though highly
embellished. At all events this one was considered worthy
of note, by the promoters of the said magazine, which at
that time was considered as one of the early attempts to
educate the popular mind.

The reply brought against its truth by the other
captain was, that he had seen, and taken up out of
the sea, great long shaggy pieces of seaweed, 50—100
feet long, which, when tossed about by the waves, had all
the appearance of a great serpent; for which this one
might have been mistaken.

Another subject of discussion brought forward was
the actual height of waves in a storm. I have heard
it said by old sailors that no wave is ever more
than fifteen feet perpendicular—that is to say from a
dead level. Allowing fifteen feet for the rise of a wave,
and fifteen feet for its fall, would make thirty feet of
apparent height from top to bottom of a wave. An observation however was made of a case that far exceeded this.
Two midshipmen were in the cross-trees of the mainmasts of

two line-of-battle ships, one in each, in a violent storm;
and they observed that when each vessel was at the
same time in the trough of the waves, they could
neither of them see the other. Allowing that seventy feet
is the height of the mainmast of such a ship, 55—60 feet
must have been the elevation of the wave between them
at the moment referred to.

These discussions, however, as to fact and fiction, served
to pass away the time, though at the cost of the respective combatants. There was on board the vessel a
party of Germans, another of Portuguese and of
Spaniards, and a small one of English, the steamers
not being so full of passengers at that time of year.
Each party exclusively kept to itself. We took on board
two Spanish priests. The one looked sour, sallow, cun-
ning and suspicious. He seemed evidently to have
practiced seclusion, and perhaps maceration; with a
good deal of the gloomy *fur atque sacerdos* about him.
The other was a perfect contrast—wrinkled and aged,
but active and courteous in manner. He wore a small
black net cap, instead of a hat, that was continually
falling off, and was as often picked up by some one
else, and blandly offered to him, at which he seemed
highly pleased. There was also a portly Portuguese
baroness, and her daughter, who looked more like her
sister, and who gave herself great importance, which
seemed granted to her by her countrymen. And last,
not least, there was a tall mulatto female slave, dressed in
white muslin, mixed with light grass-green, that "varie-
gated," as some one said, the group amazingly. In hot
countries the women are never skeletons. They are

prone to obesity, as they never walk out in the streets, which is neither considered fashionable nor pleasant.

The captain was a good sterling specimen of a British sailor, who seemed to consider it professional to take an observation, in cloudy weather especially, if he could, and appeared to desire to attain the climax of mathematical accuracy in so doing. At all events, by the help of this and the patent log, it was decided that we were speeding along at 290 miles per diem. The vessel's postal contract being only for a rate of nine miles an hour, the coals in this swift vessel could easily be saved by working only one set of engines; or we should have gone faster.

Two petty thefts took place on board, to the great disgust of the older seamen. Investigation brought it home to two new hands, who were placed in irons, and consigned to water and bread of affliction, in the hold, until the vessel touched land. The folly of such misconduct ought to have been apparent: for not only did these men lose their pay, but they were left ashore in a strange place; and, as the names of such offenders are invariably entered on a black list, they were prevented from getting occupation again.

When we were 450 miles from the African Coast the vessel and all parts of the rigging were covered on the larboard side with a very fine brick-red dust. This has been decided by savants to come from the Great Desert of Africa, which at this stage of our voyage was 800 miles away; and it is the fine _débris_ of vegetable matter wafted by an East wind.

I heard a captain say, that when he was first a sailor, and in the main-top for some hours, he saw from where he was, a black line on the sea approaching from the horizon till it passed the ship, and reached across to the other horizon like a black band. It was a vast shoal of porpoises, many abreast, migrating; and as they were passing for several hours at considerable speed, they must have comprised many millions.

CHAPTER II.

WE were now fairly in the tropics ; and as we advanced, the full heat of a vertical sun compelled us to remain under the awning all day. The evenings were comparatively cool and delightful. The moon and stars, from the rarity of the atmosphere, seemed to radiate a bright light that we never see in England; their outline being crisp and distinct; and whenever it lightened, there was the same superior distinctness. At night a French steamer for Bordeaux passed us, her red port-holes in the dark being only visible. The customary " how d'ye do" and "good-bye" were exchanged, in the shape of a blue light and a rocket, from each vessel. Few and far between seemed to be the visitants of this vast ocean expanse. At times the feeling would strike you of risk, in being so many days out of sight of land, and sailing on water three miles deep. No events varied the scene, excepting the rolling over of whales, as they pursued their course one after the other, and the deck being covered with flying-fish at night, attracted by the lights, thereby affording us a fry for breakfast

on the following morning. They were about the size
and colour of a small mackerel. Once I saw a dolphin
coursing after a flock of these little fish, alternately leaping
out of the water, and plunging forward after them, seem-
ingly with its mouth open, enjoying the sport.

WHALES.

On January 21st, 1868, we passed the line, under which
there are generally, if not calms, breezes and showers,
with which we were favoured rather heavily, and which
caused the glass to recede from oppressive heat at 85°
to 72°. The heat, owing to this cause, was 10° less
than it would otherwise usually have been under the
line. So that, having passed across the mighty Atlantic
with a quiet sea and mild weather, we might well congratulate ourselves.

The first land we now saw, 260 miles from the Coast
of America, was Fernando di Noronha, the penal settlement of the Portuguese Government. It is remarkable
for its striking perpendicular rock, 1000 feet high, the
pinnacle alone being one-third of that height.

The Coast of America, as we now approached it, seemed
very flat. A long dark streak distinguished the shore, which
is lined with dark cocoa-nut trees, for three-fourths of a
mile from the sea, all along this coast. These trees will not

grow unless they have a sea-breeze. I was surprised at being told that for 3000 miles of coast, excepting the large cities, the land is a pathless forest, uncultivated, and unowned by anyone, and without native inhabitants.

FERNANDO DI NORONHA, AS SEEN FIVE MILES OFF.

The first place we stopped at was Pernambuco, which is 8 degrees south of the equator. The city is low, and is protected from the ocean waves, which roll in here with unmitigated force, by a natural breakwater of sandstone that runs all along the coast. Our vessel drawing 22 feet of water, could not enter round the pier into the harbour. There was a tower at the entrance of it, and houses crowded behind it. The dark cocoa-nut, the palm-trees, and bananas that covered the slopes from the harbour, with the canoes of the natives, hollowed out of the trunks of trees, and guided by black naked negroes, gave the scene a strikingly tropical appearance. Heat and moisture combined seemed to produce a wild, rank, gigantic vegetation, for which the vast Amazonian wilds are so noted.* Altogether, our countrymen seemed like fish out of water in a country like this, where every man you meet is jet

* One palm-tree grows with leaves 25 feet long and 6 feet wide.

black, and where little clothes are required, or worn. Off the coast we saw what are called rattans, which are a sort of boat of three planks united together, with a thin iron rail round the gunwale, having a lateen sail with which to run close to the wind, sailing quickly, and carrying large loads of fish. We soon started for

BAHIA.

This city and port is 380 miles further; and I was astonished and delighted at the sight of the people and the place. The coast the whole way was lined as before with the cocoa-nut and the palm; and on rounding the hill fort at the entrance, we steamed straight up the harbour, which appeared to be about ten miles in length and breadth. The city of Bahia extended along our right side for four miles; and, as it faced the sea, it had a noble appearance. There were large quays and landing-places, lofty merchants' houses mixed with others of greater pretensions, continuing up the hill, surmounted with the towers of churches, for 250 feet above the water.

We anchored a mile and a-quarter from the market-place; and, landing there, we beheld (a most striking scene) an assemblage of the finest blacks and mulattoes that, it is allowed, can be seen in any part of the world. They were almost entirely in Eden's dress costume. All of them were slaves, and as happy and merry as possible—magnificent specimens of humanity. I stood, and admired a black Hercules, who was loading some heavy iron, for ten minutes, and could hardly leave him. An anatomist would have been lost in admiration of the biceps, triceps, deltoides, latissimus dorsi, and all the rest of the animal motive powers here to be seen. Michael Angelo, in his wildest flights of imagination, could never have portrayed—in his frescoes of struggling, frantic Herculi, writhing in masses together—the human frame better than it was here displayed in its more ordinary labours. Perhaps that celebrated painter came here to take a forcible lesson from Nature. Men and women alike were far above the average as to height, and, the latter especially, as to weight. Some of the women were like fat, black porpoises. I watched one huge creature continually eating. Her great lips and vast mouth seemed capacious enough to swallow everything at the stall—pumpkins, baskets, and all. "It was like shovelling coals into a cellar," as I heard a stoker say. Everything quickly and easily disappeared.

I turned from this offensive mass of obesity; and who should pass along but a tall, thin black girl, *very* scantily dressed, with a short sky-blue skirt, and hair like a mass of wool piled on her head—no false chignon!— on the top of which was a basket. She was the nearest approach to a skeleton imaginable, with hardly any calf to the legs; doubtless the effect of disease. The contrast between what I saw and had just seen was so great, that I was fairly obliged to take off my hat, and laugh immoderately into it, in the street. All were happy and jolly to a degree. Talk of slavery! It would be a privilege for any Dorset or Somerset labourer to be half so well cared for, and as careless, as all these people seemed to be. Talk of curates with large families in England, or Welsh rectors with £60 a year! They would envy the slaves here. No whipping here, I thought, for that fat would never bear it!!

The women were fantastically dressed with coloured turbans and petticoats, and a shawl drawn tightly round the hips, and tucked in, their dress being of every variety of bright colours. One half of the breast and back was covered with a thin scarf; the other half was naked. All were dressed differently, and were decked with necklaces, bracelets, and armlets of gold, that made them appear altogether, with their many-coloured dresses, the most picturesque and singular people that I ever saw.

Slavery must have been a profitable business formerly, of which these are the existing remains. It is now professed to be both impossible and illegal to run a cargo. The gain of a successful disembarkation of slaves must have been great, quite counterbalancing the loss of nine ships out of ten. A slave would cost about one pound or one pound ten shillings on the Coast of Africa. Here he is worth £100. Much has been connived at by the subordinates of the authorities in past times, when bribery was more openly resorted to. Doubtless many have perished, but chiefly from cruelty and deprivation on the African Coast, not so much from the voyage; it being the manifest interest of the slave-merchant to take care of his cargo. So much for the past. One thing is certain, and that is, that you may buy a slave here now for £100; and you may hire one, or let one out for "an ounce a month"—about three guineas, or £38 per annum; a pretty good interest on the investment. Many slaves have redeemed themselves, and been enabled afterwards to purchase others. It is a common thing for a master to permit his slaves, male or female, to go out on their own account day by day, and earn what they can more than at the above rate per day : the surplus they faithfully bring home to their master, and leave it with him to pay for their redemption.

The slave trade was prohibited by law in 1850, with the approbation of the whole country, and severe measures were passed against it ; so that the traffic may be said to be extinct now. The Government do not in any way acknowledge colour as affecting civil rights ; nor does the feeling of the people give it any weight as regards social standing. There is here none of that insolent contempt which is shown to negroes in the free States of North America, where a negro is turned out of an omnibus, in New York, as unfit to sit with white citizens. Any slave can avail himself of his privileges here. He can go before a magistrate, have his price fixed, and purchase himself. Some of the most eminent men in the country are Africans, and have distinguished themselves as students in the medical, legal, and theological schools. So that Brazil may be said to be a very Paradise for negroes.

Every one that I met, except English and Portuguese merchants, and their clerks, were slaves. No lady ever walks out into the streets, but receives visitors in the evening. Her slave sits at her feet during the day. I saw at the entrance of one house four female slaves lying asleep on the mats outside the inner door ; and three at another. The ladies sit in their upper rooms, and a slave sits on the verandah. As our party passed by one house, the slave evidently told her mistress, or the young senoras ; and a rush was made to the windows to see us. They seemed very much to admire one of the party—a handsome young clergyman—and kissed their hands to him ; which

enabled us to joke him pretty freely, by asking him who his
friend was. In the market there were several beautiful
marmoset monkeys, the smallest of their tribe, generally
secured by a band round the loins to the necks of the
women they belonged to. When hanging, the younger ones
especially were like large spiders. Even ladies carry them
in their bosom; for they are very tame and delicate.
They live chiefly on bananas, and almost invariably die
on board ship from cold. The price asked for them was
equivalent to two shillings apiece.

Immediately we landed we set off for a walk, as the
manner of Englishmen is, to explore the city, regardless
of a climate so different to a temperate one. Two of our
party chose to do things in style, according to the fashion of
the upper ten thousand of the place, by taking their seats,
amidst our facetious congratulations, in the Sedans of the
place, which were very different to those of Beau Nash's
days. Fancy a sort of basket car, not much unlike a
cradle that would be suitable for an infant giant, with a
small canopy over it, and side curtains, of a sky-blue colour
with large gilt stars upon it. A pole is run through it,
not to transfix the luxurious occupant, who sits with one
arm over the pole in the inside, his hat in hand, the
image of patient fatigue; and he is carried by two tall
Golcondo blacks up a steep hill for two miles, in the heat,
for about one shilling. This seemed to be the usual
conveyance for gentlemen returning to their homes from
their business. I thought the fare cheap. Englishmen
and especially Scotchmen, with their peculiarly thrifty
propensities, are fond of cheap things. I fancied I
should have liked to have taken the place of one of the

blacks, merely to have ascertained what was the amount of the labour in such heat : but I was satisfied when I saw the two blacks suffering apparently as intensely from the primeval curse, as Englishmen would do ; mopping their faces after their exertions. Only, unlike Englishmen in like circumstances, they took a glass of clear water, at the top of the hill ; and seemed satisfied.

On the quay the heat was like a furnace, and I should think 140° in the sun. We slowly ascended the steep street of the city that runs up obliquely, and parallel with the harbour, for three miles to the public gardens, which are on an elevated spot, with terraces from which we looked down on the whole harbour and shipping. The entire slope of the hill was covered with every sort of wild herbage and tropical trees. There were avenues of tamarind trees and bread-fruit trees, widely extending, the bread-fruit of the latter hanging under the branches, as big as a man's head. At the gates, as we went out, the avenue terminated in splendid palm trees, the trunks of which swelled out just above the ground, and then ascended narrower up to the heads, which were flattened out into a fan-like union of the stalks of the leaves, which were two yards long. The flowers that had burst from the pods were hanging in a long white cluster, over which the pods remained expanded, as if to give shelter.

Such trees as these it was clear could not possibly exist, with their gigantic luxuriance, except in uninterrupted heat. There were light scarlet and yellow butterflies that shot past us with the speed of birds, which were four inches wide across the wings ; though there are some moths double that size in this country. Then there

was a spinning sort of buzz in the trees over our heads,
caused by large flies, that ended their song in a prolonged whistle.

TREES IN TOWN GARDENS, BAHIA.

At the side of the garden were aviaries, with rare
pheasants, and black and scarlet birds, and others of
very gorgeous plumage. I picked up some tamarinds
and found one occupied by winged ants with red heads,
half an inch long. We partook at a confectioner's of
copious libations, of various colours and tastes, on our
way up and down this hill, and gladly so from the excessive
heat. Certainly the city, as we viewed, it with its monastic
edifices, its site, harbour, and shipping, and its strange
occupants, was a splendid place. We met several mule
four-in-hands as we returned, the livery of the servants
being a pale green, which gave a faded appearance of
style to the appointments.

Everything here seemed to be performed by manual

slave labour. Inside the merchants' offices there were placed on the stairs stout poles for the blacks to carry heavy boxes with, and even large casks of wine. A large cask, perhaps weighing a ton, was rolled into the street from a warehouse. Ten blacks—six behind and four before—slung this cask on the middle of two poles. They all raised it at the same time; and crowding their shoulders and arms together, to divide the weight, they proceeded to carry it between them, staggering along, while they kept time with a curious responsive yell from one to another. Their arms and legs were bare, and they wore dilapidated straw hats, canvas jackets, and very short breeks. They seemed not to feel the labour, and did their work with comparative ease. It is clear there were no carts or waggons to be had, to do such work.

Altogether I paid a most agreeable visit to this strange city; though I found the glass was standing at 96 under the awning, and 85 in the cabin.

February 1st, we took leave of Bahia, and commenced our next course of 733 miles to Rio. Divine Service was held each Sunday on the voyage; the captain summoning all the crew and officers on deck, and then marching them down into the saloon, around which they were placed. If a clergyman is on board, he performs the service; otherwise the captain reads the Church Service and a sermon after it. A few of the foreigners attended. Some that were on deck seemed curious to know what we were about; for foreign Roman Catholics are taught that Protestants have no sacraments, or creed, or religious worship, and are only heathens; and consequently they class them as infidels.

We now looked forward with anxious expectation to behold Rio, the wonder of the world for beauty and grandeur of scenery. The coast assumes a lofty and mountainous appearance, long before you come to the harbour. A succession of lofty peaks, lost in the distance, are seen, backed by a higher range of mountains, which are the Organ mountains. A shoal of porpoises made a dash at the vessel as we neared land, gamboling and turning over : ten of them took their station, side by side like a row of soldiers, close in front of the cutwater of the ship, and kept there for a long time, though it was going at the rate of twelve miles an hour. The rest of them frisked about, leaping over each others backs, going down to a great depth, and shooting up again.

As we entered

RIO HARBOUR

the hills on each side were deeply indented with chasms, the hills and rocks between rising to a great height. There were little bays between the lofty rocks, with sand at the water's edge, and a row of guns in embrasures fortified the entrance at each one of these places. There were several islands outside that put me in mind of those in the Lake of Killarney, with their dark and bright green shrubs, and grey-tinted and red rocks beneath.

The sugar-loaf rock, rising out of the water 1500 feet perpendicular, stood at the left entrance of the harbour, perfectly precipitous on all sides but one, and that almost inaccessible. Some of our young midshipmen however managed, in joke, to plant the Union Jack on the top; and the natives had great difficulty in ascending the rock to pull it down again. A lofty walled fort, like one of

the Sebastopol forts, with several tiers of guns, is built
on a flat rock on the right side entrance which it guards,
rising as it does almost from the water edge. There
are several pointed rocks 2000 feet high just above this
fort, and beyond it, inside the harbour, between which
a line of guns are placed, as before, in embrasure. In
fact this part of the harbour is a focus for the fire of
all the artillery stationed around. For just within the
entrance on the left side is an island rock strongly
fortified. No ship is permitted to pass this fort, on its
passage outward, until it has been examined. Any of
the inhabitants of Rio wishing to depart, must publish
their intention in the papers for three days before, lest
they should leave the city in debt. When they arrive at
this fort, and pass examination, a signal is given from it
to the outer fort; and the vessel is then permitted to go
out to sea.

The striking beauty and magnificence of the landscape
all round, that breaks upon you here, is unequalled.
Imagine a dozen bays of Naples, as many Vesuvii
mountains, and some König-sees thrown together, and
this will give you an idea of Rio, its harbour, and
neighbourhood. It has well been called the wonder of
the world. Sydney harbour is like it, but very inferior.
Its singular beauty consists, not in bare Alpine rocks,
but in the combined richness and grandeur, and yet
softness of the scene; every hill having herbage, shrubs,
and wood, to the top; and every valley being rich in
tropical luxuriance. There is nothing sterile or uniform
here. The hills are most varied. Peak after peak, some
with flat volcanic-looking tops, succeeding each other to

the most distant perspective, convince you what endless beauties of nature there must be in the whole country.

Beautiful bays indented the harbour on both sides, between the mountains, some had rows of houses facing them with avenues of trees, each little bay looking something like an English watering place. On the south, or left side ranges the city of Rio, with its 300,000 inhabitants, on its very irregular site; for it seems intersected almost everywhere with bays. Islands, and promontories stand forward into the harbour, with lofty tropical trees, ancient monastic buildings, nunneries, and mansions, overhanging the water and crowning their summits. I positively came away without sketching any one of the magnificent views that struck me, both from sea and land, from the ship; for while each one was worthy of being had in remembrance, the eye was lost in the multitude of their beauties.

The city extends by the water side about five miles, winding into the different indentations. The harbour is about twenty-five miles long, by from five to seven wide; and it is studded with islands. At its farther end the land rises in broken masses of grassy hills, terminating beyond them in the distant Organ mountains, which raise themselves to the clouds in a long and lofty outline. Some lofty rocky peaks rise in front of them, which are supposed to be like the pipes of an organ, from which the hills take their name. The most notable conical hills on the left, as you enter, are Tichuga, 3600 feet high, the Corcovada, 2400, and others of nearly the same height. The harbour has numerous flag ships stationed there, and vessels of all nations are congregated;

those that are stationary having awnings spread over their decks, and their port-holes left open, to keep them as cool as possible in the great heat. A great many small steamers were moving to and fro, across the harbour, there being several small towns on the side opposite the city : so that the scene was not wanting in animated as well as still life. Altogether it forms such a combination of everything that can constitute earthly magnificence, that it is considered the *ne plus ultra* of the world.

CHAPTER III.

WE slowly steamed up the harbour for about three miles,
and were boarded by the officials of the Customs House,
and by officers of the different men of war, for news from
Europe, &c., &c. And then we took up our position
at the coaling island, as it is called, a mile and a-half
from the landing-place in the city.

Here we see what it is to be hoped are the last remains
of slavery; and they give any one that witnesses them an
idea of what slavery must formerly have been, in its worse
forms. A gang of fifty slaves were employed to remove
a pile of coals from a platform into our steamer. The men
were most scantily dressed with very short canvas drawers,
and a shirt of the same material, but more like a waist-
coat. Each man had to carry coals of about fifty pounds
weight in a basket on his head; and before he passed
along the plank into the ship, had to step once on an
iron slab, as I suppose to register the proceeding.
They commenced at five in the morning, and left off at

eight o'clock in the evening, and were perspiring at every pore from the intense heat, which they certainly seemed to feel far more than I should have expected for natives of the very hottest clime. Their black skins at a little distance had a frosted look, which was from the drops of perspiration standing on the surface. It is curious that the Red Indian nations under the equator in South America show a constitutional dislike to extreme heat, which proves they must have been strangers and have emigrated into such hot regions, to which their constitutions were not originally adapted, and that they have not since become perfectly acclimatized to it. It is the negro alone who is the true denizen of tropical regions, to whom intense heat seems natural. I asked where the " Whipper in" was. Properly speaking there was none. But the slave master stood there with his whip, which I was told he seldom uses, and that when a slave is refractory he is generally taken before a magistrate to be punished.

I learnt that the slave gang were locked up at night in a row of barred cells, which are guarded outside by savage dogs, that have the range of the whole of the little island, to see that none escape. These blacks were certainly inferior in physique to the Congo blacks of Bahia, which are the finest race of any. It took half a day more for these men to embark the 900 tons that the steamer required. I was greatly laughed at by the captain of our ship, and by the proprietor of these slaves, for saying I should like to have had a cask of English beer to distribute among them. They certainly did their work well, and without flinching, and doubtless must have been well fed. Though I perceived

that working as they did in the sun, with the glass
standing at 130, they were covered from head to foot
with perspiration, and seemed almost to feel the heat
as much as I should have done.   It is an undoubted fact
that these negroes are, in intellect and in the moral sense,
far lower than our race.   But it was a melancholy scene
of human degradation to witness human beings in whose
nostrils the Creator of all has breathed the breath of life,
and given a reasoning soul, locked up in dens, at night,
like so many brutes, and guarded by dogs.   "Old England
for ever" thought I ; for it contrasted strangely with
the romance of everything that met the eye around.

We took boat to the main landing-place, near the
Customs House; the houses on the pier had a row of
trees in front, as you often see in England.   A new
dock was just being opened by the Emperor of Brazil,
and a crowd was assembled to meet him.   I waited to
get a good view of him, as he passed by me.   He looked
like an intelligent English gentleman, grey headed, and
in ordinary costume; and he seemed to walk without
concern among the people (by whom he is highly esteemed), with no military or police attendants.   In
political matters, as the head of a liberal republican
monarchy, I fancy he has little actual power.   The
ghost of such a thing as a king is, however, useful as
the visible organ, a mouth-piece of the wishes and laws
of a free people.   His title is Emperor; and he is well
suited to his people, and deservedly beloved.

The first object we were recommended to visit was
Tichuga with its falls.   We approached it in a carriage
drawn by four mules (in fact it was an omnibus), for six

and a half miles, along a valley that receded into the lofty hills. At the extremity of this there was a steep zig-zag road, like a macadamized one, and lit with gas-lamps for five miles up the steep ascent, to a sort of platform, or saddle, between the mountain of Tichuga and an opposite hill. At the foot of this ascent we were obliged to exchange the carriage for saddle-horses. As we had to walk our horses, we preferred taking the old rough road which went straight up, and which was like the rocky bed of a torrent; and we found that we had kept pace with a carriage on the trot up the zig-zag that joined this road on our left side. After walking our horses patiently up the hill, when we had surmounted the ascent, and looked back, we were rewarded with a fine view. Each side of the valley we had ascended was covered with flowering trees of every variety of colour, the lofty hills rising to a vast height on either side; and, looking back, we saw the road by which we had come winding down, and along the level ground beneath to the city, with the harbour and distant mountains filling up the landscape.

A nice hotel received us for a hearty second breakfast, and we descended another winding road over a saddle of the hills into a valley where the Tichuga river, that rises in the mountains above us, finds its way down; and here it falls over a large barrier slab of rock, about 45 feet high and 100 feet broad, which is called the "falls." At this time, it being very dry weather, there was only water enough falling to cover the face of the rock; but in heavy rains, when there is plenty of water running, the fall, from its height and width, must be very imposing in appearance. A succession of pointed mountains, about

3000 feet high, bounded the landscape here on either side;
and pasture lands in the bottom, extending to the sea, terminated the view in front. All down the valley were scattered
here and there great boulder rocks, that had fallen from
the hills above, with little cots and gardens between
them; black women were washing their clothes in the
stream, and little naked black imps were playing about in
groups; while the papa nigger was sitting up to his neck
in the water. The conical hills above us were very sub-
lime, the scavenger-vultures and buzzard-hawks soaring
round above them. Here and there, over the sea, was
flying the frigate bird, so called because he pounces upon
other birds when they have fished up anything, and makes
them give it up.

We returned from our survey up the long ascent again;
and after refreshing ourselves with excellent provisions
at the inn we descended into Rio, down the smooth
winding road. I heard that it was kept in the state it
was, and lit with gas, from the number of merchants
having country houses on the elevated platform of this
hill. After devouring several ices, we walked to the town
gardens of Rio, which are very much like the usual gardens
of that sort, only that all the trees are tropical, the broad
flat-stemmed palm trees being the most prominent. There
was a long raised esplanade that joined the sea on one side
of these gardens, the waves breaking against the wall. It
made a nice promenade, as it gave you a different view
across the harbour, and all around. The smells from dead
matter in the sea were very offensive here.

The gardens have a long canal-like piece of water
running through, or rather round them, which contains

a unique rarity called the peixe-boy or ox-fish, a species of fresh-water seal brought from the Amazon, the only one I was told that is known. Its peculiarity consists in its having no mouth or teeth; its mouth, properly speaking, ending in a long pointed snout with thick lips round it, resembling very much, in this respect, the great ant-eater. It is very tame, and readily comes to you. We invoked its appearance by shaking a piece of paper on the surface of the water, which it came to and sucked. It is about eight feet long; and seems to like sporting and rolling over like a seal. It is partly black and white in colour; and certainly is a great curiosity. In the city I met a seedy-looking individual on an equally wretched-looking horse. He was a beggar. Beggars on horse-back are no proverb here, but a common reality. And as I stood at the door of a shop, four men carried a sick emaciated man, who was lying on a sort of palanquin couch with curtains round it. He also was a beggar. These cripples fatten on the righteousness of almsgiving—as Romanists conceive those good works of theirs to be, which a false faith teaches them will secure heaven. At night, returning to the vessel, the heat was so insupportable, at this hottest period of the year in Rio, that I took a pillow and blanket on to the deck, and slept on one of the seats for three hours—a most dangerous thing to do, even though it was under the awning. I was told that though you may be under the protection of this awning, a most dense dew settles on everything, and a fever, which is fatal in a very short time, is almost certain to ensue, as the pores are so open from the heat. It commences with an intense chilliness and chattering of the teeth.

c

The following day we proceeded to

THE ROYAL BOTANIC GARDENS.

This place is five miles from the centre of the city of Rio.
We approached it in an omnibus that runs on a tramway in
the street, drawn by mules.   It had no pole, but a wooden
drag or lever pressing on the wheel, that the conductor sat
upon when necessary to stop to pick up passengers.   We
were set down at the termination of the rail in a pretty
square, with good houses around it.   At one side of the
square was a fine church, with the two usual massive towers
at the side of the main entrance, which all these foreign
churches have.   In the centre of the square was a large
lawn, round which was an avenue of fine palm-trees and
walks ; on the lawn were " umbrella trees," well answering
to the name.   This tree is short, with leaves like a laurel,
only much larger, and its branches spread widely on every
side, which, with the seats under it, afforded a capital shade
as well as rest.   The heat was so oppressive that we found
it only possible to crawl along slowly, with an umbrella to
shelter us from the sun's powerful rays, and were glad to sit
on these seats when opportunity offered.   For the rest of
the distance to the gardens we took a mule cab.

The gardens themselves, both as to their site, as well as
trees, were very beautiful.   As you enter there is a lodge
at each side, with a broad walk to the right and left, and one
directly in front.   Each of these walks are lined with lofty
palm trees, eighty feet high from the ground to the leaves,
and are allowed to be the finest palm avenues in the world.
We explored these gardens in every direction, through the
different walks.   In some places there were large clumps
of bamboos growing in damp spots, and various trees that

we had never seen before. Running about, quivering, in every direction, were lizards of all colours, which we chased, but could not catch; the exertion only aggravated the excessive heat from which we suffered so much, this day being moreover allowed to be, by the inhabitants themselves, the hottest day in the year.

What adds to the singularity of this spot is the vast pinnacle rock of the Corcovada, which rises here, a sheer precipice from the gardens, 2400 feet high. Several hills and peaks, that would appear astonishing anywhere else, were around these gardens, and some more distantly in other directions. Insect life here seemed profuse and vigorous. Butterflies almost as large as the palm of the hand, some white like paper, with almost transparent wings, flapped slowly about in the manner that our white owls fly over the bushes. Others, part sky-blue and part black, though lesser, with bodies two inches long, like the bodies of savage beetles, swarmed in every direction. At the fall of a stream to which we ascended were various sorts of humming birds. One, like a minute magpie, black and white, with a long tail, fluttered upright before the walls and rocks in search of its prey. While another little bird, like a small bronze meteor, flitted past, poising itself upright in the air in front of a flower, into which it stuck its beak, the humming sound certifying to the ear the rapid vibration of wing by which it supported its tiny form in the air. Greatly delighted with this strange place, we returned exhausted and thirsty, and could hardly restore ourselves with plenty of tea and ices.

I was kindly invited to the country residence of an English merchant not far from the city, only situated at the other side of the hills, in a valley approaching the Corcovada. This enabled me to visit the mountain on foot, and see the wondrous view from the top of it, which is an unequalled sight, and perfectly indescribable for its splendour. I first surmounted a short steep hill, and then descended on to the aqueduct road, which winds round the hills into the city.

THE ASCENT OF THE CORCOVADA.

The aqueduct runs along a lofty ridge of hill, with a carriage road at the side of it. Proceeding along this for three miles, I reached the tanks, built across a narrow valley, in the hills where the water is collected, that passes down this narrow enclosed watercourse, and supplies Rio with water. Passing this, I reached the winding mule-road that leads to the top of the Corcovada. Instead of taking this road, which would have made the distance longer, I followed the old rough, direct ascent, which intersected and crossed the mule-road every here and there. In this unfrequented track I disturbed several large green locusts, four and a-half inches long, that with difficulty fluttered to the boughs of the bushes, under which they remained suspended. Some had orange-coloured tails the same length as their bodies. Their wings were partly a dark green colour, and partly orange. I found also "the stick insect," about eight or nine inches long, that leaped away from me two yards. It had three legs on each side its body, being like a slender stick supported on wires. The lofty trees above me were inhabited by different tribes of monkeys which were signalling to each other as I passed underneath. I should have missed seeing these insects, besides many other curious things, had I been on horseback on the winding road. And I have generally remarked that travellers on foot see much more of a place than those who go by a conveyance.

I was much exhausted with the first hour and a-half's ascent, as it was very steep. I luckily arrived at a large mushroom-shaped erection, thatched, with a table round the centre upright, and benches and seats, which had evidently been provided as a refreshment or pic-nic place for visitors. To rest myself I laid down on this table for twenty minutes, gazing at the solitary wildness of the forest around me, till I caught myself almost napping. I then started up and paced on, with my coat on my arm and umbrella overhead, for an hour more, making two and a quarter hours, at three miles an hour, from commencing the ascent. And I was glad to find a refreshment place at the foot of the last winding ascent, which, for 500 feet, is very steep to the top. Here I procured a bottle of Ind and Coope's beer for two shillings, and some inferior bread and cheese; and, like a giant refreshed, I valiantly reached the top.

It was a fine clear day. Even the Organ mountains had no nightcap on them, which they so frequently have. Everything in the vast terrestrial expanse of the landscape was clearly and distinctly defined, to the most distant hills, from the dry state of the atmosphere; and from the same reason the distances were very deceiving. A short thick wall surrounds the small platform on the summit of the Corcovada, which is hardly perceptible from below. And here you might, in looking down and around, imagine yourself transported to an "Arabian Nights" scene. The sight was so gorgeous, it was astonishing. You could peep

over the perpendicular precipice of 2400 feet on the upright
side of this rock, to the botanic gardens below that I had
visited the day before. You could see the different merchants'
houses scattered along the roads, looking less than pins' heads;
valley beyond valley, and hill on hill surmounting one another, crowned beyond by the more distant but far higher
cones of Tichuga and other peaks, some having flat tops, and
terminating the landscape south and westward, in distant
succession. Beneath was the harbour with its shipping, and
islands in beautiful variety, every part of the landscape different, and yet contributing to the whole. You could look down
into every bay and fort on the opposite side; and the eye
could trace up the several valleys, until lofty hills limited
the view. Here you perceived the vast height of the Organ
mountains better than from below, 8—10,000 feet high;
and yet, though nearly fifty miles off, looking quite near.
The forests that clothe the summit of the Corcovada, and
the cultivated aspect of everything—its inhabited appearance, from the number of houses that are scattered about
in every direction, and that line the little bays and crown
the promontories,—added greatly, in contrast with the
Alpine scene, to the beauty of the prospect. I could hardly
tear myself from this matchless spot; but as it was past five
o'clock, and I had seven miles descent home, I was forced,
though I again and again returned to it, to depart—never
to see such again. What a traveller has said is true to
the life—" The first effect of tropical scenery on those accustomed before to the gloomy leaden colouring of our northern
clime is so dazzling, that it appears to us impossible any
other place in this world can be so perfectly beautiful, and
beyond description, either in prose or verse, as Rio."

At night, and especially from being in the suburbs, we could not escape from the annoyances that are peculiar to a hot climate. The frogs made a continued loud chirping, one appearing to be the chief speaker, while the rest repeated the din, until you were wearied out. Doubtless their notes conveyed ideas that were understood by them, but they were so often repeated (as people meeting at home make observations about the weather) that you knew what the last speakers would say as well as the first, until in half-sleep the noise seemed like a pulse beating in your ear.

HOUSE SPIDER IN BRAZIL—ONE-THIRD THE SIZE.

Mosquitoes, of course, find you out and creep in at the smallest opening left in the muslin curtain; and after you have exterminated every one inside, and you think you may be at rest, the same buzz and twinge awaken you. You strike a light, and administer the like destruction to them again and again; till fairly worn out at last, and driven to sleep, you are obliged to resign yourself to the mercy of these blood-suckers; and in the morning you find your forehead, wrists, and back of the hands marked with their bites. Just at early dawn, *"Ecce iterum Crispinus,"* as Horace would say; and a startling nuisance begins in a loud, ringing, metallic whistle, which is taken up and prolonged all down the valley by some large flies in the trees; sounding just like, and quite as loud as, an English railroad whistle, leaving off with a scream. This is repeated at intervals until the sun is fairly up, in its heat. These insects, I am told, burst themselves in singing against each other.*

Before leaving Rio we heard disastrous accounts of cholera in the southern parts, that fifty a day were dying in Monte Video. Changing to a smaller vessel, the Arno steamer, of 800 tons burden, in consequence of the large ocean steamers drawing too much water for the River Plate, we resumed our passage without meeting with any peculiar incidents except a Pampero storm, and a renewal of sea-sickness from changing to a smaller vessel; and we at last arrived at Monte Video.

---

* People are apt to call this country "the Brazils;" which is a wrong expression. It is never so called in the country itself, any more than India can correctly be called "the Indies." To do so is almost as bad as the name given it by a poor old woman I once met with, who told me she had a son come home ill from abroad. Her reply to my inquiry was, "He was a *sodger*, and had been *wounded* with a *bagonet* in the *Brass-heels*."

CHAPTER IV.

THE city of Monte Video lies at the north entrance of
the estuary of the Plate. The river is called Plate, but
pronounced Playte, Plate being Spanish for silver—" the
silver river." The city is approached in shallow water,
which loses its blue sea colour for many leagues before
you get near it. Some sand banks about here are
dangerous for shipping. The river is in no place more
than nineteen feet deep, although it is 150 miles wide
at the mouth, yet, from the vast amount of mud brought
down from the great rivers Parana, Negro, Paraguay,
and their confluents, it abounds in shallows. It is continually running seaward at about three miles an hour.

The harbour itself of Monte Video is of a horse-shoe
form, with a small conical hill on the left side as you
enter. The city, with its 80,000 inhabitants, is built on

a hill on the right of the entrance; with the custom
houses and warehouses on the lower parts adjoining the
quay. There were about 1000 vessels in the harbour,
none of any size. The national guard ships were lying
out from five to ten miles off.

As we approached the landing-place there seemed to
be a great deal of excitement among the people; while
the flags of different European nations were hoisted
over the custom houses and chief buildings. It appeared
that Edwardo Flores, the son of the president, had seized
the fort which lies at the lower part of the city near
the water, with some of the troops, and had just before
been compelled to evacuate it, by the French and
English, who had restored it to Flores again. This it
will be seen connects itself with what shortly occurred.

I stayed eighteen days in Monte Video, and saw many
things that gave me no prepossessing idea of the place or
people, nor of the governments of these South American
cities. In the first place the cholera had made, and was
still making, most frightful ravages. The accounts also
from the city and camp of Buenos Ayres were awful.
In that city people were carried off by thousands; 18,400
having been computed to have perished in it. Nearly
half the inhabitants of the city had fled into the camp
there to avoid it. In that camp it became even worse,
in many places no one being left to bury the dead; and
pigs were eating the bodies. Sheep, cattle, and horses
were scattered over the whole country, their owners
having all perished by cholera. Numbers of children,
whose parents had died, were found crowded together,
in a starving state, in the sheep corals. A gentleman

who had been there told me that flocks of sheep had been offered him at fourpence per head, so great was the terror that had seized the people living there. A total, with those that died in the city, of 70,000 deaths was reported; though the exact number can never be known.

In Monte Video, where upwards of 4000 died, the heat was very great, and the doctors were called up at night many times to attend persons who were seized with cholera and were dying in every direction. You could see every morning placed at the corners of the streets the clothes of persons who had died in the night, which, having been set on fire, were still smouldering, in lots of three or four, scattered about. Tar barrels were burnt in every street by night, to dissipate the infection. There seemed to be with the natives an extreme reluctance to take the remedies that were prescribed; and by a strange infatuation they prevented medicines being administered to their dying relatives. And this was independent of the great unwillingness to take any means of cure that is so peculiar to persons that are seized with cholera. No vegetables or fruit were permitted to be sold in the market; and no fish was eaten, as it was supposed to have fed on the floating carcases of those that had died of the cholera. I heard afterwards of an Englishman in the camp having been asked to take out of a poesta, or shepherd's hut, the corpse of a person who had died from this complaint, because the natives themselves were afraid to touch the body. They offered him "an ounce" to do this—about £3. 2s. He accordingly got upon his horse, opened the door of the house, and threw in his lasso round the neck of the dead man in bed. The horse then hauled out the body, and it was dropped into the grave prepared for it. For this disease is contagious, as well as infectious.

In the midst of this frightful scourge that existed in the city of Monte Video a revolution suddenly took place.

At two o'clock, on February 19th, as I was returning from a walk through the streets from the westward part of the city, I saw the people evidently communicating something to each other, and others running in an excited manner, hurrying to close their shop windows. At the same time I heard repeated musket firing in the direction of the fort.

The political parties in the country had been for long divided into two factions, the whites and reds—Blancoes, and Coloradoes. A conspiracy had been formed by the Blanco party, both outside and inside the city, to oust the Coloradoes, and bring in their own representative, it being now the time for a new election to the presidency. Tidings of this had secretly reached the Government about a week before I arrived, and because Flores the president disregarded and disbelieved it, his son Edwardo had taken upon him to seize the fort to protect his father from the adverse party. It is to this that I referred in mentioning the excited appearance of the city on my first landing.

The plan of the conspirators outside the city (headed by Berro a former president when the Blancoes were in power) was to assassinate Flores, and seize the Government. Their attempt first commenced by the sending up rockets, as a signal, outside the city, and murdering all the Colorado ~mandoes in the country round it. The Blanco party

then proceeded to seize the cabille, or town hall, on the
west side of the Plazza, or city square.   Part of the garrison
in the fort were Paraguayan soldiers; and these had been
bribed by the Blancoes to rise and join them.   But
the Government having tidings of this, had had them
removed to another place the evening before.   When
the governor, Flores, who was at the fort, heard that
the cabille had been seized, he set off by himself in his
carriage to go there.   Three sets of hired assassins were
placed, one in each of the three ways by which Flores must
approach the Cabille, and which they had concluded he
would do.   One ambush was an unfinished house that I
had passed only five minutes before.   And as Flores came
by, the conspirators rushed out, shot his coachman and
horses, and stabbed him to death in his carriage.

Berro, the leader of the Blancoes, went with about a
dozen of his party to the fort to seize it, expecting the
Paraguayan soldiers there immediately to desert to him
and join him.   He shot two of the soldiers that opposed
him, but was soon mastered, with his party, some of whom
succeeded in escaping by a boat to some vessel in the harbour.   Flores' son, Edwardo, who was quite a youth, came
up to Berro in the fort, and without suffering him to
excuse himself by saying that "if he had not taken the
lead, his own party would have assassinated him," nor
permitting him to divulge who his confederates were
—first embraced Berro, who was a fine old grey-
headed and mild-looking man, and had been his former
friend; then, drawing back, he drew his revolver
and shot him dead.   So much for style in Spanish
tragedy.

...dent was much beloved by his soldiers, ... the people. The news of his death ...rrison in the fort, who immediately ...cable to take it, firing up the streets ...o clear them of the people. Noticing, ...where I lived, several persons peeping ...the street, I went out to see what was ...were coming up this street from the ...among and just then a gentleman ...the street was shot through the ...case. A peon crossing the ...head, picked up, placed on ...his I thought it prudent

...they fired volleys ...was on one side ...whole week the ...at their houses ...in the streets ...the soldiery, until ...slaughter.

Flores the president was much beloved by his soldiers, and respected by the people. The news of his death infuriated the garrison in the fort, who immediately marched out to the cabille to take it, firing up the streets in every direction to clear them of the people. Noticing, from the house where I lived, several persons peeping round the corner of the street, I went out to see what was the matter. The balls were coming up this street from the soldiers who were advancing; and just then a gentleman on the opposite side of the street was shot through the thigh, and taken into a house. A peon crossing the street at this spot was shot dead, picked up, placed on a shutter, and carried away. On this I thought it prudent to retire into the house.

When the troops reached the plazza, they fired volleys on the mob, to clear it. The cathedral was on one side and the cabille on the other. For a whole week the Blanco party in the city were routed out of their houses and abodes, and were hunted down and shot in the streets in every direction, such was the rage of the soldiery, until a public proclamation appeared forbidding the slaughter, and ordaining that the guilty party be fairly and legally tried. Twenty corpses were lying at the prison, and doubtless many innocent persons suffered. A small army of Blancoes were cut to pieces outside the city. All the English merchants shut up their houses, and business was totally closed. Every one armed himself with a revolver. No one was suffered to be in the streets after eight o'clock at night. Nothing was to be seen there but the serenos, or watchmen, — like our "old Charlies,"—with lanterns and a sword, crying the hour

THE CHATEAU OF VERSAILLES——THE PLACE OF LOUIS XIV.

of the night. Twenty-nine of the leading citizens—one being General Flores' brother—remained at the cabille all night to guard it, and in the morning they were all found dead of cholera. Thus, wholesale murder, and cholera raging on every side, made a very unpleasing variety after England.

The troops bivouacked on the grass in the centre of the large plazza; the matrise, or cathedral, being on one side and the cabille on the other. The military band was playing in the evening, and the townspeople saunter-ing up and down in the walks under the avenues of trees. The black and swarthy savage Paraguayan soldiery had lit fires, and were cooking their meat on upright spits over the fires; and the whole scene, after the butchery of the day, presented a curious aspect, the soldiery being in whitish-coloured regimentals, and giving anything but a sense of security to a beholder.

On the body of one of the conspirators a list was found of sixty-eight persons who were to have been assassinated, including the whole of the senate and two of the principal English residents.

The troops returned from the country on the 20th February, after cutting to pieces 150 of the Blanco army; and yet the same evening thirty-one of these troops died from cholera, brought on from fatigue, drink, and heat. The guard ships of the different nations sent their marines ashore to guard the custom house, ambassadors, and merchants' houses. It being impossible to leave the city, I was forced to remain and listen to the fearful accounts of both bloodshed and pestilence that reached me from every quarter. It appeared that two former

or ex-presidents, who were with the Blanco party, had
died by violent deaths on the same morning that Flores
did. An attempt was made to embalm him, that he
might lie in state preparatory to a grand public funeral;
but no one could be found that understood the process.
They had recourse to a bird-stuffer, who attempted it and
failed. The body was then put into spirits and kept for a
time, but at last was obliged to be buried without the
pomp and circumstance intended. It was computed that
about 460 persons had been killed in this affair, besides upwards of the 4000 that perished at this time from cholera.

One great drawback to a residence in South American
cities is undoubtedly these unpleasant revolutions that
periodically prevail. When a revolution occurs, it is
generally at the expiration of a period of three years
(which was the time that this took place), when a new
president has to be chosen. Interested parties then strive
to get into power, at the cost of money and blood, in
a most reckless manner; their own advantage, and that
of their friends (not that of the State itself), being their
only object. Hence, constituted as these liberal republics now are, without a substantial middle class to
secure order and peace, such things must be expected
continually to happen: but as these nations advance,
these things become less pregnant and less dreadful.
In some of these states, where one individual usurps the
power, and has the army with him, he becomes the most
unscrupulous and blood-thirsty tyrant conceivable. No
atrocities that have been perpetrated in any age or place
in the world, from Nero and Domitian, can match those
committed by some South American autocrats, who have

been monsters without one redeeming spark of generosity about them. Lopes, in Paraguay, as one among many, is a comparatively mild instance. When Rosas was expelled from Buenos Ayres Presidency by the help of Garibaldi, he had not only in times past executed in cold blood numbers of his supposed enemies in his reign of terror, but there was found a long list of Englishmen whom he had doomed to death.

One thing is certain, which is, that money can do much in this country in the way of gaining a presidency. Flores, himself, whose death I have here related, over-turned a previous government of the Blancoes, or white party, and landed to commence it with *only two* soldiers. Every man in this country is liable to be taken to serve as a soldier; and he is promised pay which he never gets, though the officers *are* paid: consequently, on the first opportunity he deserts, and never shows any desire for fighting. An army of 800 men was once levied in the Banda Oriental Camp; and when they returned each man to his home, not one had been killed, and only one was slightly wounded. But if money is provided and paid in hard cash, it then becomes a very different thing. It has been surmised, and has yet to be disproved, whether Flores, on the occasion I refer to, was not considerably helped by the Monte Videan Banks; they having a promise from him, given them, of the power of unlimited issue of paper money, to a far greater extent than their real capital, which has left them in their present insolvent state now that the day of reckoning comes. Of course I here speak only from surmise, which, if true, will account for much that is otherwise inexplicable.

There was one thing that struck me with regard to these bloody revolutions, and that is, that bloodshed seems customary in an excessive ratio, and is less thought of in countries where the Roman Catholic religion exists, there being in reality no actual punishment for homicide as a crime against morality. Any murderer in these countries can free himself from even arrest at once by offering to enter the army or the police. Of course where there is a priesthood that arrogates to itself the power of forgiving sins of their moral guilt, this greatly diminishes the supposed crime of homicide, and reduces it practically to a very little. And as government policy also unites with this, the result is, that the criminal invariably escapes, as there is no death punishment in these liberal republics except for political offences.

I had no wish to stay longer in Monte Video, after what I had experienced there; the *foreign* society also (namely the English) that I met with was neither very attractive, nor on a par with that of Buenos Ayres; the upper ten thousand of the latter being far superior in position, refinement, and morale. As a proof of this, I may mention that bull fights are still perpetrated at the former of these cities on stated occasions.

Being invited to stay a few days with an hospitable merchant in Buenos Ayres, who has a keenta, or country residence, outside the city, I availed myself of his kindness, the steam voyage there being only 120 miles from Monte Video. The shore of the south side of the Plate, as you sail up the estuary of that river, and on which the city of Buenos Ayres stands, is excessively flat and unpicturesque. The great drawback of this broad part of the Plate is the extreme shallowness all over the river, caused by the continued accumulations brought down by the great rivers that supply it, from the extensive interior of South America. The effect of this is, that from twelve to fifteen feet of water is the usual depth, and also that the wrecks of ships abound; the part opposite Buenos Ayres having many sunken vessels there which the Government is too lazy or too stingy to remove. Ships above 300 tons burden are compelled to lie out eight miles from the city, and smaller ones two and three miles, the unoccupied water between distinguishing the respective tonnage of the crafts.

The city, with its 250,000 inhabitants, is entirely built in squares of a hundred yards each side; only, unlike English squares, the walls of the houses form the outside of these squares and join the footpaths. The roadways are most roughly paved with stones of every size and shape, and are only sufficient in width for two vehicles abreast. The footpaths are very narrow; and as no stone is to be found in this republic, the paving for the footway is brought from England, and is generally some of our old used-up paving-stones. The drainage is very bad here, which alone is sufficient to induce disease. Still it is but fair to say that, as regards cholera, it was never known in these South American cities previous to the year 1867; 1868 being its second year.

There is nothing attractive, picturesque, or worth noticing in either Monte Video or Buenos Ayres. On arriving at this latter city, you are greatly struck with the very unusual manner of landing goods from the vessels. There are two wooden piers that extend from the shore out into the water for about half-a-mile or more, made of "underwaye" posts, a hard iron-wood, that sinks in the water like iron, and is brought from the Paraguay river, where it grows. All the wood of this country is well suited to stand the climate. The deal we use in England would split entirely into bits under the scorching sun; but these dark red iron-woods will endure any heat, and are imperishable in water. .

The River Plate here is from thirty to thirty-five miles wide; and when the wind blows from the north, the water rises the whole length of the pier up to the walls of the city; but when the wind is from the south, nearly the entire length of the pier is standing out free from the water, or perhaps partially covered. In this case the water becomes very shallow,—that is to say, from three to four and a-half feet deep,—for a considerable distance out, of a mile or more : so that the sailing lighters can hardly approach the pier with passengers only. To load and unload vessels, the only resource in this state of the water is by carts, the beds of which are elevated by a second bottom, to keep the goods out of the water. The poor horses go out for a mile and more with the carts, and stand there an hour and upwards in the water, with it up to their backs, in the midst of all the shipping. To see some hundred carts and horses in the midst of as many ships for a mile and a-half from the shore is a curious as well as a cruel sight, for in cold weather these horses sometimes die in the water. If merciful men are merciful to their beasts, none such can be here. When a load is to start from a vessel, the horses rise out of the water on their hind legs and plunge, in order to move their load; and when they cannot succeed in moving it, an additional pair of horses is attached to it; a man with bare legs, standing, in Ducrow style on their backs and flogging them on their necks, and with difficulty moving the cart; the head, neck, and point of the horse's shoulder alone being above the water. Our " cruelty to animals " society ought to establish " a branch association " here; "limited liability " would, of course, be indispensable.

The city, although not noted for its piety, abounds with churches. The cathedral, which is the largest, stands in the large plazza or square, and occupies, with the archbishop's residence, one entire side of it. The churches are all of the same heavy, massive build, plastered (as there is a want of ornamental stone) outside, and white-washed, with invariably two great towers standing up on their front side. This is the universal style of build throughout every part of South America. The walls of these buildings are generally eight feet thick. In Lima, on the west coast, where from the fifth to the fifteenth degrees of south latitude it never rains, the fronts of the cathedrals and churches appear to be highly decorated with richly-carved stone; but these decorated parts are only cast in mud, which, in a country where rain is never known, becomes nearly as imperishable as stone. And as rain and storms have great influence in destroying stone, their absence in Egypt, where it seldoms rains, preserves the monuments of antiquity in all the richness of their more delicate parts as fresh as if just from the hands of the artificer.

The interiors of all these buildings are decorated on the walls with a row of black or white images of

the Virgin Mary and Child of every size, from that of
a large doll to the size of life; and these are adorned
with tawdry flowers, lace, and finery of the most childish
character, with no pretensions to ecclesiastical dress or
effect. There was evidently a designed distinctness in
these images and their paraphernalia, one from the other,
as if a certain specific virtue was capable of issuing from
the one, which the other did not possess. Their arrange-
ments and equipments seemed to imply this, although, being
one of the uninitiated, I was unable to decipher it. Some
were more artistically manufactured than others; while
many were of the most common design and dress, and
quite a burlesque on the former. Perhaps each had a
separate vocation or office, and perhaps, also, the images of
superior mould were more " worshipful " than those which
were less artistic. Diana of the Ephesians was great apparently in more places than one. I thought, " if these be
thy gods, O Israel, to go before you," " they that made them
must be like unto them," at all events in the matter of religious worship. The only impression left upon my mind
was that it was an unsightly mixture of the blasphemous
and the ridiculous, and a most direct contradiction of
the Second Commandment, which Roman Catholics are
careful to omit altogether, and split the Tenth Commandment into two, to make up the ten, thereby setting
Exodus xx., first part of seventeenth verse, and Deuter-
onomy v., first part of twenty-first verse, at variance.
Here you see what you never can in England, because
it is cautiously kept out of sight,—the most revolting
and uncouth idolatries of Popery.

As I was passing one of the churches in Buenos Ayres

AN AMERICAN CHURCH.

at forenoon, I heard some fine voices singing; so I looked in, and as the chanting was that of fine tenor and bass voices, rather in Italian bravura style, I thought I would stay awhile. The building was only partially lit up, it being at the commencement of the service, and was appropriately dark; at least, in accordance with the idea that spiritual darkness and devotion are sure to go together. The priest was responding in Latin now and then to the voices in the gallery overhead at the entrance. A row of ladies with black mantillas knelt along each side nearest the walls, and facing the high altar; and there was also a row of old, poor people in the same attitude. Along the centre was spread a long carpet, with a row of chairs on each side, some of which were occupied by gentlemen. As that was the part I considered I ought to go to, I accordingly sat down on one of these chairs. In a short time a black acolite entered with a bundle of candles, three feet long, under his arm; and lighting them, he proceeded to offer one to each of the gentlemen on the row of chairs, and lastly to myself. Sometimes we stood holding these lighted candles, and sometimes sat or knelt, while the chanting was going on. After being thus entertained with dumb show for half an hour, I began to feel I should like to retire into unincensed air; and looking behind me to see if any one wanted a candle, I observed that all the chairs behind me had been filled up with gentlemen, each having a candle to hold. What to do with the candle I knew not. I could not blow it out, and walk out with it under my arm, much less use it as a walking stick. I did not wish to appear indecorous or irreverential, even were I in a heathen temple. At last summoning courage, I turned round to some gentlemen just then coming in, who were both chairless and candleless, and politely offering one of them my candle, I sloped out as decently as I could. I afterwards discovered that this was a grand mass celebrated in honour of some general officer in their army who had died of cholera. My presence, therefore, as a candle-bearer was a small contribution in honour of the deceased, whose name I did not know, without my either knowing it or intending it; and certainly no prayer for the dead escaped from me. " If ignorance is bliss, 'twere folly to be wise."

As to the dress of the officials, I heard that the black dress belongs to a priest; the red is for a cardinal; purple for a cardinal of the Holy College; and, at Rome, white for the Pope, signifying purity, especially as he is, at the time I write, about to be made " beautiful for ever " by assuming infallibility.

CHAPTER V.

MARCH 4th, 1868. I crossed over from Buenos Ayres
to the ancient town of Colonia, on the north side of the
Plate, about thirty-four miles distant. This town is
said to be the first that the Spaniards touched at, in
this part of South America, when they first discovered
it. It has 1000 inhabitants, and is of a very dilapidated
appearance, from having stood three sieges and bom-
bardments within the last thirty years. The ancient
town of Jan Carlos was formerly three miles to the
westward of it; and it contained about as many inhabitants. But in one of their cruel wars—"the long
war"—its occupants were put to the sword, and the houses
burnt, and overturned. A small chapel is the only
building that is now left standing there; a few ranchos, or
native mud huts, with here and there a cactus and some
orange trees, alone mark the spot where the town once stood.

All the hedges outside the town of Colonia, as well as around Monte Video, were composed of American aloes of very strong growth. Some had the flower stalks still standing. In other places gaps were protected by fixing these stalks along for fences, as fir poles are used in England, while the gaps themselves had a stout leaf chopped off the root and stuck upright in the ground. The formidable spikes of the leaves are an ample obstacle to the intrusion of cattle.

My occupation in this part of the American camp compelled me to gallop over the whole of a district of about · seventy-five miles from east to west, by about eighty from north to south. During the last nine months I was in it, I rode 4000 miles over it by myself, steering chiefly by the sun or by objects on the horizon. I, of course, met with a variety of incidents in my constant peregrinations, such as no single inhabitant was ever likely to experience. It, however, enabled me the better to appreciate this beautiful sunny land, and to form a more correct estimate of its capabilities, from the number of sources from which I was enabled to gather information and form an opinion. Living near the centre of this square of "camp," I had to visit six different places in regular succession once a week, besides other parts occasionally. To three of these places I had to gallop fifty miles in one day, returning the same distance two days after; and at the three other times, to stations at distances of from twenty to thirty-five miles out, and the same back.

Travellers' stories are allowed on all hands to be wonderful; that is, they will bear being interpreted *cum grano.* But, at the same time, it is a fact that it is impossible to live in such a wild country as the South American continent without meeting with things and occurrences that are almost incredible. I do not for a moment receive as true many marvellous things I was told, such as the statement made to me by a very respectable Estanziero (as he said, on undeniable authority), that the Tobas, a Patagonian nation, have their knee joints reversed, like the Centaurs of old, and are able to run as ostriches do. Nor do I believe that there was a man in the camp who had a horse that was born with only one fore leg, and that it grew up and could gallop like other horses. Either instance of these two, if they could be produced, would be a valuable prize for Barnum's show. And such, reduced to a reality, might have somewhat of the effect that Dr. Livingstone mentions was produced on the mind of a native African, when he brought him to the sea and he saw ships for the first time; the result being that when he went on board a steamer, he was so wonder-struck, that he lost his reason and jumped overboard. But I am prepared to believe from occular demonstration much that I would never have believed had I not seen it.

I believe in the account I heard from a major in command in Oude, in India, that there are there what go by the name of wolf children. That is, that when the wolves steal the native children, though they generally eat them, yet in some cases they bring them up as their own progeny: and these children learn to run on all fours, and bark and snap like the wolves themselves. And that in the Province of Oude there is an hospital for the reception and recovery of such beings when they become adult. This is stated by Colonel Sleeman, in his "History of Oude," and is attested to by so many credible witnesses, that, however singular it may be, I am *expected*, if not forced, to believe it.

It is clear a distinction must somewhere exist between the credible and the incredible; and our error will be in being too incredulous as regards the former, or too credulous as regards the latter. Experience only will elicit the solution of these things.

Many of my readers may be acquainted with the following anecdotes, which I here repeat for those who have not heard them. A Red Indian came, as deputation from his tribe, to General Washington, the President of the United States; and when he went back to his tribe he told them of the marvellous things he had seen,—the ghosts, spectres, &c.,—and they believed them all. But when he told them, among other things, that he had actually seen a canoe carried up into the air by a bag of wind, and kept up and moved about there, they were so convinced he was telling them an untruth, that they altogether disbelieved him, and put him to death for practising an imposition on his tribe.

A Japanese king was told by one of his people who had travelled in England, that water in winter became solid there; and he said it was so absurd and impossible that nothing should induce him to believe it. And generally any man who has discovered what is strange is looked upon as a sort of intellectual harlequin,—as a knave, a fool, or a madman, or as a mixture of each. So was Harvey derided as guilty of absurdity by the whole medical profession of Europe, when he discovered the circulation of the blood; and Galileo was thrown into prison, and would have been tormented to death in the Spanish Inquisition, and was laughed at by all the then Christendom, because he affirmed the discovery, which every one now knows to be true, that the earth revolves round the sun, and not the sun round the earth. Herodotus states that some Grecian and Phœnician sailors sailed round the Cape of Good Hope, and that when they came back they declared they had seen the sun at noonday in the exact north; on which his comment is, "Any one that likes may believe this, but to me it is impossible and absurd." And so it is that scientific mistakes always bring more derision and discredit than any that are made in a science that is not an "exact one."

I now proceed to the description of this country, which was the site of my travels. And first, I would observe that the ancients had a knowledge of the country about 2000 years before its discovery by Columbus, which is clear from what Diodorus relates of the Phœnicians, of whom he says, that when "sailing beyond the Pillars of Hercules they were driven by great tempests far into the [western] ocean, and being tossed about it many days by the violence of the storm, at length they arrived at a great island in the Atlantic Ocean, which is many days' sail distant from Africa to the west. The soil was fruitful, the rivers navigable, and the buildings sumptuous." By which we conclude that it must have been peopled long before.

The best way to form an idea of the vastness of this continent is to place a map of it before you, and to bear in mind that it is about 4000 miles from north to south, and about 3000 from west to east, and that a space of 100 miles square will bear much the same relation to its whole extent that a sixpence laid on a dinner table does to the table. You then see how little a day's gallop of fifty miles bears to the interminable extent of this country in journeying over it.

The population of the continent is supposed only to be 22,000,000, while Europe, that is half the size, has 350,000,000. In Peru alone there were 8,000,000 when first discovered, and now not quite 1,000,000.

Remembering then, when viewing the map, that the smallest parts of the rivers denote the higher parts of the land, and the wider parts the lower, you see that the great intersecting rivers are the chief outlets for drainage; and as hill and valley succeed each other all through Banda Oriental up to Paraguay, till the higher elevations become stony ridges, the traveller in this country must expect to have numerous rivers to wade. The higher north you travel into the Paraguay country, the more mountainous become the upper parts; and in some parts are fastnesses, very sparingly inhabited. The montes, or river-side woods, become more extensive; the climate far hotter; and savage animals of the larger kind, as the jaguar and the largest eagles, are very numerous. An African sportsman might find Paraguay a pleasing change if he wished for a diversified range of shooting ground; and the facility of reaching it would be a great inducement after experiencing the difficulties of passing through the fever beds of mid-Africa, besides having to pay native African chiefs for permission to pass through their thickly populated districts.

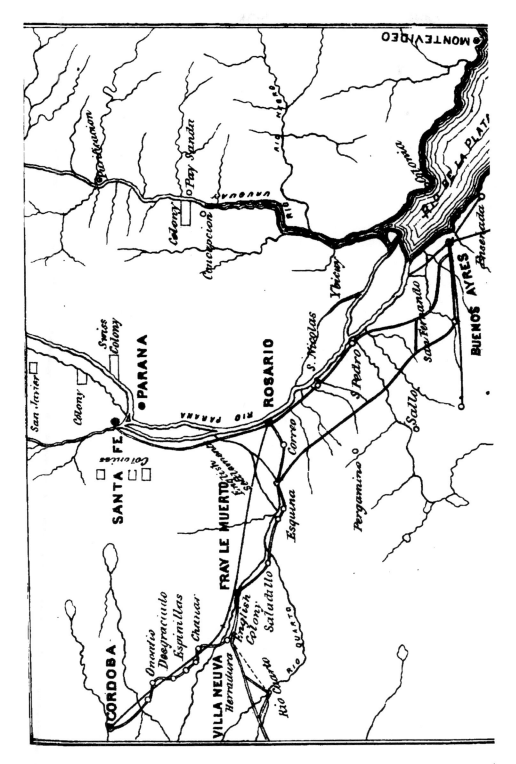

To the westward of Banda Oriental comes "Entre Rios," the rich lands between the rivers Uruguay and Parana; and westward of this again extend the fertile plains intersected by the Argentine Railroad running across that part of the country, where small lots of fine land are to be procured at a moderate price, the access to it being most easy and least toilsome. And as the land at the sides of this rail is becoming quickly populated by English emigrants, a settler here is by no means so secluded as to intercourse as he is in those wide fields so scantily occupied in other parts.

The Buenos Ayres or south side of the River Plate, is a dead flat for hundreds of miles; but the north side, called Banta Oriental, with its capital city of Monte Video, is entirely undulating in ridges of hills (cochillo's), with rivers or small streams between them. It is also very thinly populated; not one-fifth as much as the country on the south side. It is entirely a pasture country, without trees, except the solitary omboo, growing by a rancho, poesta, or estanzia, which serves as a landmark; and such woods that are there are invariably by the sides of the rivers. The largest trees are a sort of withy, very like ours; the tala, a sort of laurel; and a vast variety of flowering bushes, with nearly all of them long thorns. These form dense thickets; and if you are washed down into them in fording flooded rivers, it renders it difficult to get out of them.

When travelling, in crossing rivers, you must always be careful not to attempt doing so except at a regular pass (for there are no bridges in this country), or you

may easily be irretrievably bogged in four or five feet
depth of mud, in the narrowest caneada or ditch. It is
not sufficient to see marks of cattle having merely gone
down to drink on your side of the stream, to enable
you to pass it safely; but you must also see marks
of their having emerged from it on the opposite side
also. *Sand* and stones in the water is a sure sign that
it is a hard bottom. It is desirable to avoid crossing
rivers, which are often very wide in a flood. And you
will often see crosses put up in trees where bodies have
been found washed there after a flood.

The sides of rivers, especially at the passes, are, more
or less, an aceldama of dead animals and of the bones
of the departed tenants of the plain; sometimes you see
an old dead bull blown up with putrefaction, or the
skeletons of others with one horn of the skull standing
upwards, and the other fixed in the ground, all the
flesh being cleaned off and dissipated into thin air by
the actions of commadrakas, flies, insects, and evaporation; so that it seems as if every animal retired to die
on the river bank—perhaps from thirst on these occasions.

You enter the river, carefully keeping to the tail of the
stream, where more silt is washed down, and it is
consequently shallower. As the stream deepens, you at
last kneel upon the saddle. The horse may have to swim
only in the middle part of the river, though in floods it
will be often from one bank to another. In which case
you sit down on the horse with the water to your chest,
and you must on no account check the horse, but leave
the bridle loose, as the result would be immediately to
drown him, for nothing drowns so quickly as a horse.

THE AUTHOR ON HIS GATTEO (CAT-COLOURED) HORSE.

As you thus swim, especially if the flood be swift, should
the horse turn the wrong way, you must smack him on
the neck with your hand, or dash some water at him on
that side, to turn him straight; and if the distance
across is too great, and you find it too much for him,
you must slip off behind him, hold on by his tail, keeping well back, and he will be certain, thus relieved of
your weight, to draw you to land. From the violence
of the " temporals " and thunderstorms here, the rivers will
rise many feet in ten minutes. The water is very
muddy; and, at such times, it is not by any means free
from danger. The passage of these rivers, in woody
places, is sometimes also " enlivened " by deserters pop-
ping at you as you cross, especially in war time; such
places being convenient spots for robbing travellers.

Some make light of swimming these rivers; but, no
matter how strong you may be, and how good a
swimmer, many lives are lost from the difficulties connected with it. A young Indian officer, a Mr. Peel,
came here, who professed to make nothing of swimming
Indian rivers, which are perhaps more open; and he
lost his life here, though he had been warned against
attempting to pass in a deep and rapid current. He
was by himself; and his horse, with the saddle, returning home without him, led to a search being made; and
in three days his body was found. He had a revolver,
five barrels of which were fired off afterwards, proving
how perfectly waterproof the ammunition was.

The native population are Spanish Indian; Spanish
being the universal language, except in Brazil, where
Portuguese is spoken. You sometimes meet with an

D

Indian who retains his native tongue; but the Indian nations who possessed and inhabited all this part of the country at the early part of this century, have all retired, before a more civilized race, to the interior. Their peculiar habitat now is the "Grand Chaco" or great native forest and plain that extends up the centre of the continent from Patagonia to the Amazon country. The natives of Banda Oriental are properly a mixture of Spanish and Indian; and sometimes with a very strong touch of the negro. They are very dark, but not black; the mouth, nose, and hair shewing signs indicating the preponderance of the blood of each respective race. The Spaniard has long black curly hair and good features; the Indian has long straight hair, high and prominent cheek bones, pointed chin, deeply sunk eyes, and no beard or whiskers. Some of the figures in the Crystal Palace are correctly like them. Where there is a cross of African blood, it will appear in one or more features—lips, nose, or woolly hair.

As to weapons, the old English Brown Bess is frequently found among them. With the nations in the far interior, spears, and bows and arrows, are used. One nation uses very long bows, with arrows five feet in length. I could not imagine how arrows of this length could be drawn; but I found they were employed by this particular nation for shooting wild turkeys. The men lie on their backs when the birds get up, and, putting their feet on the bow, with the long arrow between them, pointed upwards, they draw the arrow, with the string, to their chin, and shoot the birds as they fly over them. The real Indians that you meet with, in small parties, on

GROUP OF INDIANS.

their travels, sell herb medicines and poisons; and steal whenever they can.

The only tracks across the country as a guide in travelling, are the bullock-cart tracks from Colonia (from which the wool is exported for shipment to Europe and North America) to the different estanzias or sheep farms; but in spring, when the grass grows over them, they cease to afford you any help. There is no travelling on wheels here, with the exception of the carriages and spider gigs, of North-American manufacture, that some Estanzieros use; but these are not common; everything is done on horseback. Horses are so cheap, excellent, and abundant, that any stranger riding through the country, to visit it, may be found in horses only for asking for them. Heavy things, such as logs of wood and carts, are " sinched," that is, hauled here and there where required; and the poestero hauls home his allowance of meal and yerba, &c., &c., in a box placed on the fork of a thick branch of a tree. The pole of a cart is of American cedar, and massive; and it is fixed in the centre of the cart; an iron bar stands up at the end of this pole, with a bend in it at the top. The horse has a broad cow-hide belt round his body, with a large iron ring on it, to which this iron upright is lashed; or to which a log (to be hauled home) is fastened with a strap of cowhide. It is a common thing to see a native on horseback, with canvas saddle-bags before and behind, filled with china plates, loaves of bread, iron things, clothes, and a spit lashed along the side of the horse; and yet going along at a canter. Tell a peon to fetch anything a hundred yards off, and he asks for a horse in order to go to fetch it.

A man, in short, is never seen on foot; and if on foot, birds and animals look upon him as something unaccountable; and they will come close to him to see what he is. If an eccentric *foreigner*—that is, an Englishman—were to go on foot, he would be regarded as a prodigy by everything living. The country abounds with wild cattle, in herds of 500—1000; and if they see you walking, they will come round you—their heads up and ears extended—with signs of the greatest astonishment, until, having sufficiently satisfied their curiosity, they toss up their heels and galop off. I have been surrounded with them on foot, and been obliged to discharge my revolver to keep the bulls from too near acquaintance. Small lots of most beautiful and stately mules have also come about me, showing more than curiosity, for they would have smelt me; however, the slightest mark of defiance was sufficient to keep them at a distance. The old and solitary bulls alone are vicious. There are wild asses here, very like zebras, in form and speed; but they will never let you come within 200 yards of them.

The South-American three-toed ostrich (Rhea Americana) abounds here in all parts. It weighs from 50 to 60 lbs.; and is one third less than the African, which weighs 80 lbs. It is of a dull grey colour, except the breast, which is whitish, with black on the coverts of the wings; and more so in the male bird. While the feathers of the African bird are worth £30 per lb., the entire skin of one here is worth only a dollar. They are often brought up tame at the estanzias, but always resume their wild habits at ten months old. I have galloped at full speed, and a tame one we had would run by my side, and take a biscuit out of my hand. It is curious in winter to see them running about right and left, with the speed of a greyhound, shaking out their feathers and wings, to warm themselves.

A story is told of an Englishman, who, having some distance to go, thought he might set climate at defiance; though the relaxing heat makes walking here impossible. Instead of doing in this country "as the Romans do in Rome, or the Turkeys do in Turkey," he determined to travel on foot; soon, however, overcome with lassitude, he laid down on his back and began to reflect—with one leg over the other knee. While so doing, he became an object of admiration to some Rheas, who proceeded to investigate him with the excessive curiosity that is supposed to be peculiar to weak minds. They closely surrounded him, to ascertain what he really was; or, perhaps, whether he was a biped, like themselves, who had gone through a transmigration of souls, and now appeared in his present form. Each time he moved himself he presented a new field for elucidation; and they eyed, inspected, and seemed to compassionate him the more. Raising his head, he saw there was a background of wild cattle, equally curious to know what he was. It was not till he fairly sat up, that the noble form of the British lion scared these impertinent creatures away—when he thought it time to resume his journey.

Here and there, in the boundless plains, you meet with Cardo or thistle beds, of half a mile to a mile square, which have to be avoided, from their prickles, when they are strong. Having tap roots, their presence denotes very deep soil; though being very watery when young, in the spring-time they are not healthy for cattle to eat. In spring, these thistles have large flowers the size of an artichoke, of a brilliant light blue, that tints the whole plain. The stalk stands four feet high; and, when dead in winter, being of a woody nature, it is good for fuel. When the flowers turn to seed, they supply food for thousands of doves, green parrots, and other birds. All over the country there are little owls, in pairs, called " burrowing owls," inhabiting holes three feet deep in the ground. They sit close together, very connubially, at the side of their holes, into which they vanish with great rapidity as you come near them; or they perch on the top of a thistle. They see perfectly well in daylight. Their face is ornamented with a black moustache; and as you gallop by, they flutter over your head, screeching at you.

The omboo is a very striking tree; not a timber tree,

OMBOO, OR VEGETABLE TREE.

but a vegetable one. For about a month in the depth of winter it remains without leaves; in summer its foliage is in formal clumps, and these are fringed with small white flowers, that turn to a seed like a small pea. The shoots and young trees are very stout and coarse, and spring up with great quickness. The tree is of a spongy nature, like an old cabbage stalk, and will not burn in the fire. Old trees are invariably hollow. Those in the sketch are of great size, capable of holding several men within them; and their appearance is like that of old pollard English oaks of great age; but they are not a tenth of the age that they look.

The ants build their nest about two feet high off the ground, and often around a thistle. They are a terrible pest to those who cultivate any garden ground, for they will eat down everything green often in a night. They will find their way everywhere, and seem to prefer having a nest under the kitchen fire-place. They have runs even under the narrow rivers, sinking down from high up on one bank and reappearing at the same level

ANTS' NEST AND BURROWING OWLS.

on the other side of the river. The nest is five or six feet wide and three deep, with roads to it all round, for forty yards distance, on the surface of the ground. This large ant is the "leaf-carrying ant," each one

carrying a small green bit towards the nest. They
seem to know the difference between right and left;
for those approaching the nest in a long row pass the
others on the right hand, according to the custom of
London streets. The way to destroy the nest is to dig
it out and mix it up with water into a paste, when the
sun soon bakes it as hard as a rock, and the ants all die.
Providence evidently provided, as the natural remedy for
this pest, the ant-eater, which is now only found in Brazil.

The whole establishment and active work of ant-life
is directed to one main purpose,—the growth, continuance, and spread of the species. Most of the labour
performed by the workers has for its end the support
and welfare of the young brood, which are the helpless
grubs. The true females are incapable of attending to
the wants of their offspring; and it is on the poor
sterile workers, who are denied the office and pleasures
of maternity, that the entire care devolves. The ant
community is a wonderful organized system of division
of labour. The workers are the chief agents in carrying
out the different migrations of the ant colonies, which
are of great importance to the dispersal and spread of
the species. The successful *début* of the winged males
and females likewise depends on these workers. It is
amusing to see the activity and excitement that reign
in an ants' nest when the exodus of the winged individuals takes place. The workers clear the roads of
exit and show the most lively interest in their departure,
although it is highly improbable that any of them will
ever return to the same colony again.

The swarming, or exodus, of the winged males and

females takes place in February, in a morning after a shower of rain, and after there has been no rain for some weeks. Everything is then covered with these ants. They float about the air like snow flakes; and you see them swarming about the chimney-top of a poesta, or end of a galpond, thickly covering it. The poultry ascend these buildings, and fill their crops almost to bursting with the insects. Then a change takes place among them as the day advances; for they have the power (I presume when their marriage affiances are settled) to get rid of their wings, which they do by suddenly jerking them off; and you find two pairs of narrow wings, about an inch long, lying scattered about on the camp in every direction, not shed from the roots, for a small portion is left adhering to the thorax, but where there is a natural seam crossing, at which the wing readily breaks when the insect has no further use for it. The ant is thus endowed with wings solely for the purpose of flying away to pair with individuals of other colonies, and to disseminate its kind; while the functions of the wingless class, which are of no sex, are directed to promote this, and to nurse and defend the young brood.

So that these three classes — males, females, and workers — may be looked upon as types of a much higher state of beings in the order of Providence,— young gentlemen and young ladies under the tuition and chaperonage of maiden *ants*, guiding to a successful issue our race into the haven of matrimony,— a strong instance of "development" not even perhaps contemplated under the Darwinian system.

The natives are remarkably hospitable and polite. If you ride up to a dot on the horizon, which is a native rancho, and ask the way, the native will stand facing the way you have to go, and extending up his hand and arm he will pass it down in that direction, which is very significant. It implies that you are to mark a certain spot or object on the horizon, and carry your eye on every object down to your feet. You then are to gallop in that direction without moving your eye from the perpendicular line he has given you; and so on to further horizons. You require to keep your eye carefully on this line of march, especially in crossing the streams where the banks are high, as you often have to wind your horse down into them and up out of them in the form of an S. You may thus end your crossing, if not careful, in a very different direction to the way you are journeying, and may be going at right or left angles to your route. Every brook, rock, valley, and hill are so much alike that you are easily deceived; and this error will often take place in your crossing valleys each one at a right angle, which all the while run to a centre, like the spokes of a wheel, when you imagine that they lie parallel to each other. Your only resource then is to make for some rancho and get set right; but in many places this is impossible, as you may gallop twenty miles without seeing a single hut.

Besides landmarks you have the sun to go by; and as time passes, you must allow for its moving to the west. By careful attention to these points it is remarkable to what a pitch of accuracy you can travel for very long distances by these milestones. Natives will even travel in a dark night, steering correctly by the stars. Their saddle comprises enough for them to sleep with on the ground, having the wooden "recou" itself for a pillow, and the saddle gear of sheepskin and cowhide, &c., &c., to place on the ground and over them. A gentleman stranger, in travelling, is always set forward on his journey with a complimentary escort to direct him, and often by the Estanziero himself, and the trouble of it is never thought of.

Should you require hospitality at a native's house, the etiquette is on no account to enter the enclosure in front of it without first calling out "Ave Maria," if you see no one, which means "peace be with you." In the summer heat every one sleeps during the day; and if you were to get off your horse without being invited to do so, the native has legally a right to shoot you, as the old Thanes, in Scotland, could do 150 years ago. The dogs, however, which abound at every residence, are pretty sure to announce your arrival by flying out at you. The courtesy, however, of a native you may always rely on; for he is sure to offer you the best meat he has, and a shake-down; and if you wish to continue your journey, and your horse is done up, he will freely lend you another, although you are a perfect stranger. You ask, "Will the horse return home?" (probably your distance may be thirty miles.) If he tells you to let it go when you arrive home, on the supposition that the horse well knows his way back, you let it go, on reaching your residence, at "sun-down," so that no native may have a chance of catching the "return horse" in the dark. At sun-

down, then, the horse, after being unsaddled, first takes
a roll, then feeds, and then goes in a straight line
home, crossing rivers by a way that perhaps it has
never been before, by some instinct that is superior to
man's discernment; and its owner finds it back in the
morning.

On one occasion I had mistaken my direction, and
at "sun-down," when I knew, by the lapse of time I
had galloped, that I ought to be home, I found myself,
in a dense fog, in a totally unknown place. The horse
had twice looked to the right, and I saw he knew
more than I did, though I am certain he had never
been in the place where we were; I therefore gave him
his head. He turned and carried me five miles straight
home, at right angles to the direction I was before
going. How he could do this it is impossible for me
to say, although some will even affirm that a horse can
smell its own camp.

The natives display a pride in their riches by wearing
a double row of silver dollars sewn on their broad belt,
in which hangs their Spanish knife. This pride is
also seen in their massive chased silver bits, spurs with
large rowels, and stirrups fancifully worked, with their
straps cased in silver pipes, and all of solid silver. Some
of them also have large sums of gold, in hard "ounces,"
in their houses.

As a nation they are very different to the Patagonians
or Fuegians. These last are an undersized race, filthy
to a degree, living entirely on fish, and never tasting
meat, and hating intoxicating drink; but they are fond
of smoking, and in poverty of intellect are perhaps next

PATAGONIAN AND FUEGIAN.

to Bosjesmen. No persons of great age are to be seen among them, which rather corroborates the idea that exists, that this people get rid of their older members, who are an incumbrance to them.

On the other hand, the Patagonian is great in stature, is clean in his person compared to the former, eats a great deal of meat, and drinks any quantity of intoxicating liquors, but never smokes. His gigantic stature is indisputable, notwithstanding what some may say to the contrary. Four Patagonian chiefs come regularly once a year to Buenos Ayres, to receive a grant that the Government allow them. A friend of mine, who is six feet one-and-a-half inches, stood beside these men, and he assures me that they were from six feet seven inches to six feet ten or eleven in height.

The banks, and especially the mouths, of some of the larger rivers—such as the Collia and the Sauce—are densely wooded. A camp of three square leagues, partly bounded by this river and the River Plate, was in a great measure covered with high broom. Ten years ago, when the Estanziero settled here, it swarmed with foxes, lions (that is, Pumas), and all sorts of wild animals; so that if you rode through the broom at night with ten yards of rope, with some meat at the end trailing on the ground, the foxes would seize hold of it and pull it. At night, as the Estanziero slept in his small tent (for he had no house built then), they would come and pull the sheepskin from under his pillow as he slept. Thinking it might be a native, he fired his pistol in the direction, and there was a fox dead there in the morning.

I rode along the bank of the river, which was about

150 yards wide and very deep, and, with the thickets and old dead trees, had a very wild appearance. Three pairs of eagles and some fine large falcons were sitting on the low trees and never offered to fly off as I passed close to them. I was well armed, for a short time before a lion had crossed from the other side of the river, where there is a dense forest for four miles. It killed thirty sheep in one night and fifty in another, and had been hunted out of the side we were on. The river, though large, was passable at the mouth, from the sandy accumulations, in three feet of water. This part of the river might well be called 'Rio del Morte,' or river of deaths, from forty deserters lurking there, in the extensive wood on the other side; they lived on the cattle of the neighbouring estanzias, and would kill any one that attempted to pass that way. There were two men murdered by them, just before I was there. A peon had also been murdered the day before my arrival, by another one, in revenge. I came on a fine stag, standing by its dead fawn, on which two large Coranchio hawks had just commenced feeding, while eight or ten others were waiting for their turn on an adjoining hillock. I had fully intended hunting out some lions from this district, with a large party well armed, had not illness, from the climate, and too much riding compelled me, without delay, to return to England.

A settler, who came here to commence farming, after the long war—when the whole country was reduced to a wilderness—described to me the state in which he then found it. There was only one house standing in a space of a hundred miles square, and no inhabitants and no stock. You might occasionally see a few wild horses and cattle; the dogs that belonged to the burnt-down estanzias hunted in small packs in the camp, and you were in danger of being torn to pieces by them. The settler had a narrow escape from them once, only being armed with a stick; but, by getting on a rock, and pelting the pack, he drove them away. As there were no cattle to eat down the grass, the blades of which are of a richer and stronger nature than English grass, it had grown up four feet high, under the great heat, and was in strong dry tufts. In riding through these tufts, with three dogs, they put up a leopard cat, which abounded everywhere; it was held at bay, on the top of one of these tufts, by the dogs. He rode up to it, to knock it down with his stick, when it sprang at him. The horse immediately leapt to one side, and it tore down his trousers on that side, scratching his leg. In a moment it was on the top of one the dogs it had thrown down, and it then bounded off and escaped. This shows how rapidly such a place returns to a state of nature, as the original abode of wild animals, when unoccupied and unclaimed by man.

CHAPTER VI.

RETURNING for some leagues through this wild part of
the camp amidst the thick broom to the place where I
lived, I suddenly emerged on a bullock-cart track. A
man was lying in the road; and some bullocks, drawing
a cart from the opposite direction, that was approaching,
on seeing him, had just then bolted to one side, out of
the road. Not knowing whether he was a murdered
man or drunk, I approached him cautiously and spoke
to him, and found he was a drunken Irishman, and,
with his knife, ready to fight any one. I, of course,
gave him elbow room, and passed on. I have seen
many drunken savages, in the shape, in particular, of
English runaway sailors, and have witnessed them fighting
with their teeth, and tearing pieces out of each other's

faces and breasts, because, as they said, "we are in a savage land, and must do as others do," but I never saw a drunken native nor an unpolite one; and I came to the conclusion that an Englishman, when reduced to the raw material, is the greatest savage in the world. So, at least, every English Estanziero confessed to me, that spoke on the subject; and they all said they would not take an Englishman as a peon at any price, because he was certain to be a drunkard.

I once entertained the idea that a soft southern climate, bright skies, and an out-of-door existence, naturally led to a general diffusion of kind feeling and external politeness among the lower classes, and hence that our foggy, dark, and wet climate gave this superiority in manners to continentals over ourselves. But in Norway—which is a far colder climate—the inhabitants are ceremoniously polite, especially in bowing to each other; and this is notably marked in gentlemen bowing to the poor man, just in the same way that the poor man bows to the gentleman; so that the contrary seems to be a peculiar idiosyncracy of our nation.

The natives here seem sensible of our English failing, even as gentlemen; not merely as regards inebriety, but an absence of courteous manners. Not being certain of my way once, in a wild place, I galloped up to a dirty half-naked native, and first commenced speaking to him with the early morning salutation of "Bonos dios," good day, and then I asked him the way. A strong wind prevented his hearing the first part of my salutation, when he said pettishly "Bona tarde," "Bona tarde," good afternoon, which it then was. He evidently thought I had not addressed him with the accustomed courtesy due from one gentleman to another, in asking the direction, before saluting him. I accordingly repeated "Bona tarde," and he was ready enough to show me the way, and, giving him "Gratias," I doffed my hat to him (a civility which he returned), and left him.

I must, however, allow that the savage indigenous compound of Spanish and Indian blood will crop out in all its ferocity on occasions of political excitement. In the time of war, eighteen men of the neighbouring Swiss colony, who had foolishly been persuaded to enlist as soldiers for one party, had possession of a large mill at the pass from the town of Collia, and dared not go out of it, because 300 soldiers of the enemy, who were watching them, would have killed them. At last, on the promise of their lives being spared if they gave up their arms, they were induced to come out and surrender, when twenty-five soldiers in ambush seized the mill. The others took these unfortunate men, tied their hands behind their backs, laid them in a row in front of the mill, on the grass that I have often crossed, and "cut their throats,"—their usual manner of homicide.

At another pass of a river that I used to cross, twenty-eight of the Blancoes were surprised there in the recent revolution of Monte Video; and they, after surrendering their arms under the inducement of pardon, were laid out on the grass and treated in the same way.

This faithless perfidy was defeated in a more recent case of a general who recently raised a rebellion here against the Government, and had about 1000 men with him, and threatened to take Monte Video. The army sent against him, which trebled his force, made the same proposal that he should give up his arms; but he, knowing he could not trust them, and seeing that he could not succeed, said, " No; I will retire from the country, but I will fight to the last, sooner than give up my arms." And the other party allowed him to go.

At a certain estanzia a man murdered another, and fled forty miles off. The relatives of the slain fee'd the police, who pursued and took him, and tied his hands behind him, and then deliberately cut him to pieces, the Capitas of the Policia drawing the back of his bloody knife with satisfaction through his own lips.

In time of war, when soldiers, and especially deserters, are roving about, it is not safe to travel except in a party, and armed. These men, many of whom have committed several murders, will never hesitate to rob and shoot you, if they think that they can get anything by so doing.

A settler told me that in time of war he was riding through the camp, and his peon was not far behind him, both of them having pistols. Two soldiers came up behind them. One rode in front of the gentleman and presented his musket, calling on him to surrender. The peon behind immediately shot the soldier that was behind through the chest with his pistol. The soldier in front then shot my friend through the thigh, and made off; he was, however, pursued, taken, and killed. The other soldier died of his wound the same evening. My friend was six months before he recovered from his wound.

In war time there were two soldiers who had deserted

just before from the army, in the southern part of the
camp; and they came to a small town, demanding supplies, stating that the army would soon be there.
They literally took possession of the place, levying
from the people and shops what they liked. The next
day their character was discovered, and the police pursued and took them. First they caught one man and
cut him in pieces, according to their approved method.
The other had taken off his clothes and had hid himself
under some bushes in the river, with the water up to
his chin. They took him, and in spite of his earnest
entreaties for life, tied his hands behind him, and cut
his throat.

One of these men, a few days before, had pursued an
English gentleman (who was much joked about it afterwards), prodding him with his lance behind to make
him stop while they were both at full gallop, the Englishman not being able to draw his pistol and defend
himself.

A soldier of the enemy once had been taken, and
was put to the most frightful death, by being sewn
up tightly in a raw cowhide and then placed in the
sun. The hide rapidly shrinking, slowly squeezed him to
death, the blood oozing out of his extremities. Their
positive enjoyment in shedding the blood of one against
whom they wish to be revenged is such, that while they
would never think of killing him by shooting, they would
delight in "cutting his throat." It must be a long time
before the Governments of Republics like these improve
in their administration of justice by a public and equitable
punishment of criminals, which would have a seasonable

effect on others, by deterring them from the commission of these atrocious crimes.

Foreigners who domicile themselves in these countries, or make it their adopted home, ought never to interfere in politics. If they abstain from doing this they are never molested. At the commencement of " the long war," many years ago, some English and French settlers foolishly interfered by taking the revolutionist side against the Government party. The consequence was that both French and English were carried off into Durasno gaol, and imprisoned for two years. Their estanzia houses were burnt to the ground, their horses and stock carried off, and the whole country was reduced to a wilderness.

The French and English Governments were tardy in taking up the cause of these unfortunate people; but at length they did so in earnest, after fruitless negociations. A combined fleet was sent to Monte Video, claiming damages to the extent of twelve millions of pounds, which was refused. The combined squadron threatened to lay the city in ashes; and they hoisted flags at the customs houses and chief houses of the foreign merchants, giving a short respite for an answer. On this the Monte Videan Government consented to pay four millions of money as damages, during a period of thirty-three years, for the wrongs inflicted. This lesson will ever cause foreigners settled in this country to be respected; and therefore, though there may be murders among the natives, and revolutions between parties in the State for supremacy, yet Englishmen have no reason to apprehend dangers from living in the country now. Assassinations and robberies are constantly occurring in Monte Video and Buenos Ayres that are never punished by the authorities, though they threaten to do so in very "tall talk." But such hardly ever occur among European settlers in the camp.

South America possesses many Druidical remains, in the shape of monoliths of a great size, and very perfect rock circles of both upright and horizontal stones, far exceeding in size and perfectness any in our own land. The monoliths are " Logan stones,"—the crumbling, time-worn monuments of distant ages. One which I sketched in the Piedra Chatta camp is called

THE PIEDRA REDONDO.

It is about fifteen feet high and about eighteen through. The Uruguay Republic is studded with rocky heaps piled up together, with, at first sight, an artificial look, but they are really natural. This stone on inspection proved undoubtedly to have been hewn out of the rock on which it now stands. It would not move, having tilted aside on to another rock, on which it now partly rests. It stood on the summit of a rocky ridge of hill, and had

PIEDRA MOVEDEZA IN EQUILIBRIO EN TANDIL,

much the appearance, at a distance, of a round haystack, from its yellow and grey colour.

I could gather no history or explanation of its origin from any one. Doubtless there are many Druidical remains in this pathless and boundless country that have yet to be discovered,—such as rock cities and serpentine avenues, traces of which are found at Dartmoor. There is also a rock temple, and rock inscriptions of the ancient Incas in two places in this camp; similar remains are also found in many parts of this continent, as a traveller told me he had met with no less than twenty-two of them.

But the greatest of these Logan stones, and, without doubt, the largest in the world, is

"THE PIEDRA MOVEDEZA IN EQUILIBRIO IN EL TANDIL."

This is ninety leagues from Buenos Ayres, and in that camp. This great stone rocks only from east to west, and always at the same pace, whether in a gentle breeze or a violent gale. I much question whether, when stocks and stones were worshipped, these two stones were not deified in far distant times as objects of heathen idolatrous worship, and made purposely to move by their priests, to claim the veneration of savage minds. The worship of reciprocal powers in nature, such as good and evil, seem to be natural to the heathen mind, as the mode of expressing any dictates of piety they may have. We may, therefore, expect to find that they used emblems of this in the remains of their idolatrous worship. And it is the fact that serpents, as the symbols of their devil worship, as well as the mark of the red hand, as a sign of God as the giver of life and of sustaining power, are everywhere to be seen in the remains of their decorated edifices in Nicaragua and Yucatan. And, in like manner, if we are to interpret the design intended by such rude images as vast stones, moved, no doubt, as they all then were, by the hand of the priest, what appearance could they have given to the benighted beholder but that of power and size—as of a God who possessed life. I merely offer this suggestion as to the purpose for which they might have been applied by a crafty priesthood. They must, however, have had their use, or the natives would never have taken the trouble to hew them, with vast labour, out of the rocky top of the hill, as they evidently must have done. The weight of these stones, especially the latter one, which must be some thousand tons, precludes all speculation as to their ever having been placed there and not hewn out of the solid rock on which they now stand, and of which they must once have formed a part.

There is, in the camp where I was, a rock, with deep caverns in it, that stands at a considerable height in one of the plains, which is called the " Cerro di Mala Brigos," or rock of bad neighbours, from having been the receptacle of banditti, who were a scourge to the adjacent parts. These caverns were doubtless the haunt, in former times, of the jaguar and puma, the South-American tiger, and lion, and which afterwards became used as human habitations.

One drawback here is, that soldiers, in passing through the country, have the power to call on you for meat as they go by, and to take some of your horses. In doing this, they are in some measure guided by the native police; and, if you are not friends with the police, they may take from you a great many horses. But, if you are on good terms with them, the soldiers will take, perhaps, a couple of old horses or so, which will return to you the next day, when let loose by them. These horses are required for the transport of the soldiers, and are their only means of traversing the country.

In war time, an army of 3000 men pitched their tents in a fine plain, near a large estanzia belonging to an English gentleman I knew. They took from him one morning 800 sheep for breakfast, besides demanding 200 horses, for which he, with difficulty, got a receipt, but has never been able yet to get paid for them; and if he is lucky enough to get paid, it will not be more than one-fifth their value. In the time of war, a certain Estanziero here had sixteen carriage horses taken from him by the soldiery, besides many others, which being broken in to harness, were, of course, more valuable to him than others were. A complaint was laid before our minister in Monte Video, that he might make a representation of it to the Government. He was an eccentric old gentleman who was very unpopular with the English, from neglecting their interests, in prosecuting complaints before the Monte Videan Government. The only answer the proprietor of the horses got from our minister was, " What can Mr. So-and-so possibly require sixteen carriage horses for? " and he would make no attempt to obtain any recompense for them.

But this number of carriage horses was not so remarkable in this country, where horses do not cost one farthing to keep; because, in travelling long distances, you require relays of four horses each for a heavy carriage, where there are no roads. The father of this representative of ours in this country was a medical man in England, and he composed the following verse on *his own name :—*

> "When patients sick, to me apply,
> I physics, bleed, and sweats 'em;
> If, after that, they choose to die,
> What's that to me? I Letsome!"

In a democracy, every man having the right to be respected as a gentleman, treats others the same. The sense of equality has a reciprocal influence. A republican form of government has not a deteriorating, but an imposing effect. It does not lower the higher class, but it raises the lower; and it seems to be in accordance with the order of divine providence, that all men are, personally, as regards political rights, born equal. In fact, it gets rid of roughs of every degree. A determined rough, and even an ill-mannered man is avoided by all, and is soon shamed out of his roughism. I never was so impressed as I was here, in comparison with *our* institutions, of the benefits of a republican form of government. In speaking of it as a republican, we must distinguish this from democratic, purely so; that is, it is not a kingdom where every person and thing is ruled by the more illiterate, the rude, the lawless, and the vulgar; but where every man, in the conscious sense that he possesses equal political rights, so demeans himself that he may reciprocate to others what he expects to receive from them. The idea must vanish from the mind most prejudiced against republican institutions, that you can meet with refinement only among aristocracy. You find numbers in England who live and die offensively rough in their manners; but here asperities of character and manner are soon levelled down. In this country every man knows that any amount of wealth does not constitute him *a gentleman* in our sense of the word, because he feels himself to be a gentleman already. And any sudden acquisition of fortune only impresses him the more that he has a character and conduct to sustain in accordance with his position. A labourer in England, receiving an accession of fortune, in ninety-nine cases out of a hundred, kills himself with drink. Here a man never so loses his balance. For republicanism gives a man an innate feeling of his own respectability; and it is this that makes him feel that no occupation, however humble, can degrade him. As regards American gentlemen, I can only say that I have met with most active kindness, without a speck of mercenary feeling, which I am afraid many English gentlemen, in the same position of life, are not always free from.

In South America you never see *North-*American rowdyism, which I cannot allow to be a national trait, but a peculiarity caused by circumstances in one especial class of men. A ship-captain told me he was once in the bar-room of a North-American inn, where every man wore a revolver and a bowie knife. There was a table standing in the room, and a large glass against the wall on the opposite side; and a man was standing between the two. Another man suddenly came in, who was evidently the deadly enemy of the former; for the moment he saw him, he pulled out his revolver and fired at him. The man that was fired at instantly dropped. The other coolly put up his revolver behind him, in his belt, and walked out. The people present rushed to the fallen man to raise him up, supposing he was killed, when, after a minute, he got up, as if nothing had happened. The people said, "You must surely be severely wounded?" "Not a bit of it," said he, looking carefully at the door. "Then why," said they, "did you fall, as if you were struck, and lie still?" To this, he replied, in a strong nasal twang, "I guess, if he thought he had not hit me, he would have fired again." He had missed his man, and the bullet had penetrated the glass, though it must have been a near shave. I can only say, I never heard of any such rowdyism as this in South America.

The horses in this country are compact and rather undersized, and are certainly wonderful for their endurance and good qualities, though they invariably receive rough usage. A young gentleman lately arrived in this country, after taking the saddle off his horse, gave it a fillip, to drive it away, when he was standing too near to it. The horse kicked up at him, and, with the edge of its unshod hoof, cut his throat, and he died. This occurred at an English gentleman's estanzia where I was frequently staying. Horses are never shod, and can only be taught to eat maize with difficulty. Generally they are broken in by a native, and that with the most severe beating. Their mouths also are spoilt by a powerful, heavy, and clumsy bit, with a large iron ring on it sometimes, that goes round the lower jaw, and two small rollers that press upon the tongue. With horses, lenient treatment should be the rule, severity the exception; and this only where vice and temper have to be subdued.

A "journey horse" will carry its master 80—100 miles

in a day, though it lives on nothing but grass. It is necessarily not worked hard above once in a week. If a horse is a "tired horse" (that is, has been severely over-worked once), it is never good for anything afterwards. Their pace is a canter, not raising their feet high from the ground, and, therefore, most easy to the rider. The horses here never trot; but natives, when they have a long journey to make, go in a jog trot, and they will even sleep on their horses.

The value of horses is next to nothing compared with their real goodness, £2-3 a head for compact and excellent hacks. Mares are worth from 6s. 6d.—12s. per head, according to age. They are never ridden, but are only kept for breeding purposes. A gentleman I know used to go out and shoot a mare, to get some of the delicate hide off the belly, when he wanted to form some fine plaits for a head-piece, for riding. When I first came here, I saw, at the distance of a league off, a long herd of about 800, of various colours, driven along by six natives; and, on inquiry, I learnt that they were mares being driven up to Monte Video, to be boiled down.

If you want to "carench," or naturalise, a strange horse to an estanzia, it is done by tying it to a tame mare that belongs to the place. As the strongest of the two is sure to take the other away to its home, the horse you wish secured is fastened by a halter from *its head* to the *neck* of the mare, which gives her the purchase over it and a superior pull. The treatment horses receive is in proportion to their cost. The saddle should always be tightly girthed on the back of the horse; if not, it is very likely to produce severe galls; and these sores, in the cold season, when the grass is scanty and the horse much weaker, are sure to break out again in the same place. These animals are very sagacious and docile when properly trained for lassoing cattle for marking, and they seem to anticipate the riders' wishes and exactly follow his movements. A fine climate, sun, and air, with abundance of horses to gallop over the country, is a great fascination to young Englishmen. I have often watched their extreme enjoyment of it, and have seen carried out to the very life the beautiful and expressive words of Horace—

> " Imberbis juvenis, tandem custode remoto,
>   Gaudet equis, canibusque, et aprici gramine campi."

In Devonshire the rule in travelling is—

> " Ride slowly up hill, for the beast's sake;
>   Gallop quickly on the level, for the journey's sake;
>   Ride gently down hill, for your neck's sake."

But here, for the sake of all, especially the horse, it will be more appropriate to apply the old English saying—

> " On the plain, speed me;
>   Up the hill, spare me;
>   Down the hill, bear me;
>   In the stall, feed me."

The English settlers, as a rule, are a superior and intelligent class of gentlemen, with no cobwebs of Popery or of Puritanism about them, with the usual exception to that rule of, perhaps, *one* sanctimonious and pretentious sciolist, who, of course, would be quite out of place among these gentlemanly men. I am sorry to have to add that in some parts of the camp there are sad wrecks of young men (who would doubtless be much the same in any part of the world), who always give an evil report of foreign places, no matter how good they may be.

Such men as these give way to idleness and filthy habits, and take no pains to make themselves decently comfortable, though you can see they are gentlemen by birth and education. I have gone to a poesta where smoking and expectoration seemed to be their only employment, and was told they had nothing to offer me to sit on but the skull of a cow, and where everything was as black as the dark soil of the country. Compelled to rest a night in one of these poestas, as I was once, while I lay on a mattress on some boards, I could see the stars through several holes in the roof. Very little labour, trouble, or ingenuity would serve to make them tolerably comfortable. No advantages of the country can make up in exchange for such personal degradation.

My longest gallop was 140 miles in three days, with the aid of three horses. In making this round I rested at a European settler's (who had a good estauzia), who, when a young man, was taken prisoner by the Indians and would have been killed, had not one of the women taken a fancy to him and saved him; in return for which he has been as husband to her ever since, and has now a family nearly grown up, who have the wild appearance of the Indian about them. A young Englishman in reality should never bring an Englishwoman out as his wife into the camp; the solitariness of it is so great— the household work devolving on her from the difficulty of getting a female servant—and the deprivation of what are considered in England as necessaries, are such that no Englishwoman can endure it. If a man is determined to settle down in a wilderness, let him find a help that is meet for him; and without lowering himself to take a native woman as companion for life, he can find daughters of respectable English settlers to choose from, to whom our refinements and comforts are totally unknown, and who would remain happy and contented in the position and country in which they were born.

There are no diseases here peculiar to the country; and yet I do not think that in an enervating climate Englishmen live so long as in their own land, from its wasting effects. But here death results from natural, not artificial, causes. You are not plagued to death with tax-gatherers, lawyers, or *friends,* or even with doctors, unless an accident happens. In this case the fee is "an ounce," and a dollar a league for the distance to and fro that he rides; and as medical men are very few and far between, a visit from them is a very expensive thing. Colds are unknown, and therefore handkerchiefs are the most useless part of the apparel, except to put in the hat and hang down behind as you ride, to fan you in the heat. The soft, mild climate renders living *en chemise* both possible and agreeable; and it gives a pleasing idea of what such a country must be, as regards damp and warmth, compared to England. And when, as you ride near native poestas, or on the outskirts of towns, and hear the merry laughter of children mingled with the sound of the guitar,—when you know that a dance, which foreigners so delight in, is going on, and you see the slow indolent movements of the female members of an establishment, as well as the apparent absence of want

and care for the present, or concern for the future, in
the people who seem to have all their natural wants
supplied in abundance,—what impression can you derive
from seeing this, but that people so situated enjoy as
much real happiness, so far as human necessities go, as
any people in the world can expect to do. Men of
highly refined habits may require far more than the
supplying of mere physical wants; but where the easy
satisfying of these wants—as is the case with inhabitants
of semi-tropical climes—is the chief, if not only, thing
considered, then a country like this must be as near the
ideal of human happiness as can be supposed. We have,
in fact, a Scripture sanction for describing *earthly* comforts to consist in circumstances of life like these, as is
represented by the possessions of Job and Abraham;
and that in a climate very similar.

But the solitary life of the English sheep farmer is
often apt to lead to a careless style of living, and to
indifference as to the future. And though you may have
pleasure in recalling the memories of early enjoyments and
adventures in living here, yet your powers of admiring
still life after a time become palled. The wild, beautiful
luxuriance of river-side montes, the undulating camp,
the rock-studded slopes decorated with trees of fanciful
growth, and bushes with splendid flowers, rock piled up,
with Corancio hawks and black vultures sitting immove-
ably after a debauch on the stinking carcase of a bullock
hard by, become at last tedious varieties from their constant repetition. The persevering screams of the " Teru
Teru," that chases away everything which approaches its
haunts, and even fancies it scares the galloping horseman,

E

become at length quite irritating. *Dulce domum,* lec-
turing friends, the morning newspaper, and good paved

DEAD COW AND VULTURES.

streets rise in pleasing vision before you in the silent
and solitary wearisome gallop "across camp," and "the
pleasures of memory" then seem superior to the streams
of Lethe. These passing but pleasing hallucinations are
abruptly terminated by a sudden and steep descent into
a caneada into which you have plumped down, and which
requires you to instantly wheel your horse round to
escape being bogged; and you recover yourself once
again.

CHAPTER VII.

Heat of Climate—Native Proprietors—Their Power—Compadre—Capone Dogs—Sunday and the Pulperie—Money—Native Dress—Fine Appearance—Riding Gear—Their Riding—Boys Lassoing—Skill in Lassoing—Pursuit of the Ostrich—Its Habits—Eggs—Marking Cattle—Particulars of the Process—Death of a Mare—Track-finding—Anecdotes.

IN thirty-three degrees south of the equator, in December, January, and part of February, everything sleeps in the middle of the day. Cattle and horses stand perfectly still. The sheep stand, with their heads hung down, in circles of fifty or sixty, and turned to a centre, towards each other. Nothing seems to move but the great legatoes, or lizards, three or four feet long; spiders, green lizards, and snakes,—all of which seem to be lively in proportion to the extent of the heat. People get up at daylight. If they have to travel, they stop on their journey at nine o'clock in the morning, and all sleep from eleven till five in the day. The only way of keeping the house *cool* is to do as they do in England—to keep it *warm*. They exclude the outer hot air by shutting both the windows and shutters. Not that the mid-day heat is so very many degrees above what it is in England in the hottest summer weather, but it is the unvaried heat by night that causes it to be felt so much more. The greatest heat in this latitude, for a time not exceeding three months, makes it

E 2

far more bearable than in Rio Janeiro, fifteen degrees south of the equator, or in places immediately under it. There, it is said, you feel the heat greatly the first year, more in the second, and in the third you are often prostrated by it, as the constitution has become less able to sustain it. Although, at the same time, I have met with many Englishmen who have been for a long number of years in all these places, who are as fresh as when they came out. Gradually acclimatising themselves by going home for a time, as the partners do in mercantile establishments, they are enabled to live here much more comfortably.

In a perfectly clear and transparent atmosphere, as this is, the sunsets are most brilliant. To the eastward there will be the intensely dark-blue vault of the heavens; while from the western horizon the whole sky will be lit up with bright pink tints; the more prominent clouds looking like burnished gold, while the valleys between them and the undulations are all like the same precious metal.

The natives that I met with invariably respected the English. While the Government of the country may be supposed to have been the original proprietors of the soil, yet, from grants made by it, and by the natives squatting with undisturbed possession for many years, they have become quasi-proprietors of the soil. And these men have sold their lands at different times to Englishmen. The title of land is sometimes rather precarious. When a former party in the State, as the representatives of Government, have sold an estate just previous to their being turned out, the man that has bought under such circumstances has frequently been

dispossessed by the new rulers of the country who have
come in, under the plea that the former governors had
no right to dispose of national property. This observation does not apply to the case of buying of a native,
but only of the Government. To be quite safe, you must
purchase either of a native, who has for long had possession, or from one who had legal possession long before
the new party became rulers of the State.

Many of the natives have become enormously wealthy,
so as to command the Presidency of some of these
republics; having 200 or 300 square leagues of land,
and an unlimited amount of stock, and keeping a body
of troops themselves. In some places, owing to the subdivision of land, from each child being entitled to an
equal portion, a large family will be settled with their
numerous progeny, as equal proprietors, on one small
farm; so that you will see a dozen or more ranchos,
each rancho containing a separate family. To be near
such a village is not desirable, for they are sure to rob
you of your stock. If your sheep go near theirs they
will ride round, enclosing a corner of your flock, and
drive them home with theirs; and, as your sheep will
be killed at night, recovery is impossible.

If you purchase land that has Intrusos, or squatters,
upon it, it is difficult to get them ejected: for your life
would be threatened, and perhaps taken, if you did.

To be a sponsor for a child is considered to create
such a close relationship and friendship between you
and its family, that it exceeds all other ties. At baptism
it is necessary to register the name and address of the
sponsor, because the law of this country gives such a

person the sole authority over the godchild, even beyond that of the parents over the child. This sort of religious relationship absorbs and overrides all natural ties; and to address another as a Compadre is a mark of the closest friendship. The term "compadre" applies to pairs of birds or to beasts.

A native always has a horse in good condition, even when the grass is shortest, to ride himself, which he treats kindly after it is once broken, and which is always docile, unlike the horses of Englishmen. Some of them have one or more "Capone" dogs, which are invaluable for minding sheep, and are quite as efficient as a peon at the cost of twelve ounces a year besides his keep. Such a dog, having no natural ties, is bred up with, and sleeps among, the sheep. They follow it. It stays with them in the camp all day, watches and keeps them together, and, regularly at sundown, brings them up to their rodao, or coral enclosure, for the night. I knew one Estanziero who had four of these useful Capone dogs. After bringing home the sheep he would order them to go to water; and off they would go to the river, and return in the most orderly manner to sleep with the sheep at night, and resume their daily shepherd's office in the morning.

Sunday is considered a holiday, and natives and peons forsake their occupation to meet together at a Pulperie. This is a sort of store and public-house combined, and it is distinguished at a long distance by having a very small flag on the top of a long pole or stick. The men play, for small sums, at a game by pitching knuckle-bones of sheep at a mark on the ground. Sometimes,

as I heard (though I never saw it), with the assistance
of cannia, which is a strong spirit made from the sugar-
cane, drunkenness and fighting with knives takes place
at these pulperies.

As you enter one of them, you see the shop itself is
separated from customers by iron bars up to the ceiling,
three or four inches apart, which gives the whole thing
a look of suspicion and dread, as regards customers and
the shop master. It shows he considers it necessary to
be fortified against violence. Through these bars you
see demijohns of wine and spirit, linen-drapery, ponchoes,
&c., &c., on the shelves round the shop; and what you
buy is handed to you through the bars, or through a
small door that opens for the occasion. It is possible,
however, to get a good bottle of English beer here at
a high price, and some bad cheese and bread.

The circulating medium here in coinage is, in "metallic
currency," the gold ounce of the different South American
Republics. It is equivalent to fifteen dollars; the Brazilian ounce to about eleven and a-half dollars; and the
condor to about eight and a-half dollars. The dollar is
4s. 2d. English. There are half-condors, besides smaller
gold dollar pieces. The silver dollars, the half and
quarter ones of all Republics up to Mexico, are equally
current in each Republic. The copper money is the
vintin, equal to our old penny, and double pence; and
there are silver rials, equal to five vintins. The paper
money is from half a dollar up to 100 or more, of the
different Monte Videan banks; but their value varies,
from the discount changing, according to the daily reports
that prevail as to the greater or less probability of these

rotten banks breaking sooner or later. As a rule, for this reason, the paper money is avoided in payment; and, if taken, a heavy discount is demanded, from twenty per cent. upwards. In all business transactions careful stipulations should be made for payment "in metallic currency." English sovereigns pass here at their value, being metallic; but Bank of England notes will not. The only really safe bank is the London and River Plate Bank, branches of which are in Buenos Ayres and Monte Video.

The natives dress themselves in a "cherepa" instead of trousers, which is a square cloth of striped linen, gathered up between the legs, each corner being tucked up across the thigh and under the belt. The thigh is commonly bare, as well as the leg and the foot. In riding they insert one side of the stirrup between the great toe only, not putting the foot into the stirrup at all; differing from Africans, who put the small toes only in the stirrup. Sometimes they wear long boots, but this is more as a dress costume. A heavy iron or silver-embossed spur, with a rowell as large as a dollar, is either tied on their bare foot with a thong or upon the boot. They have a light striped poncho, a sombrero hat with a broad brim, and a handkerchief on the head under it, hanging loose round the back of the head, that flaps as they gallop and keeps them cool. The sombrero is sometimes made of a rare cane that never wears out, and looks like leghorn. It is very valuable, as much as from £5 to £25 being given for these light hats. They will often be used, and descend from father to son, and grandson. Soldiers have no distinction in their dress, excepting a narrow red ribbon round their hat and a spear in their hand.

ROCKS AT RIACUELLO, AND CACTUS TREE.

AN INDIAN WOMAN LIVED UNDER THE TREE TWENTY-THREE YEARS.

Altogether, the native—galloping on his horse, with his silver spurs and other appointments, his gay coloured dress and long streaming curly hair flying back, his handsome features and gentle bearing—presents a fine appearance as the noble horseman of the plain.

In riding, natives certainly look as if they had a wretched seat, as they invariably have their stirrups very long, with the heel up and the toe pointed down; and they seem to be balancing themselves on their horse, like a forked stick placed across it. Yet they ride well. I have known a native ride after a cow, catch its tail with his hand, at full gallop, jerk it to one side, and throw it down; and before the cow could rise and escape, he was off his horse and on the ground, and had cut the animal's throat. The Patagonians, and all the Indian nations of this country, use no bits or head gear for their horses, but only a thong fastened round the horse's lower jaw. In "the Grand Chaco" the Indian women ride astride like the men, with only a single thong to the horse's lower jaw. Their clothes, of course, are next to nil.

The skill of the natives in throwing the lasso, from constant practice in catching their horses every morning, is very great. A leopard cat of the country, called "Gatter Montanos," escaped up the cactus tree in the accompanying sketch—which tree, though only a plant in England, is here as large as an ash tree—as a shepherd lad was looking for some cattle among the rocks. The lad went under the cactus tree, and threw up his lasso round the cat's neck in the tree. He then turned his horse and galloped home 400 yards, and when he arrived there the leopard was dead.

I have seen a boy, seven years old, climb up the fore-leg of a horse, and, with the help of its mane, get upon its back; then go out and lasso a sheep, bring it home, and cut its throat and skin it as cleverly as any butcher could have done.

One great sport here is lassoing the ostrich. Its speed and endurance are such, that if, with the fleetest horse, you do not overtake it in the first mile, you will not in fifty. They have some few dogs here that are crossed with the greyhound, which are sometimes able to overtake both the ostrich and the small stag that you meet with (which is equally swift), and these dogs, by biting the legs, enables the hunter to come up with his game. As the men who intend to "bola" the ostrich approach it with their dogs from different quarters, the bird's only chance of escaping is to "clear out" straight away as fast as it can, which it generally succeeds in doing. The men endeavour to get within twenty yards of it in order to cast the "bola," which consists of three round stones, one and a-half inches in diameter, enclosed in cowhide, with a thong from each stone three feet long, united together at the ends, which end is held in the hand by the hunter, and swung round over the head; the three balls, when thrown, spread out, and wind round the bird's legs.

It is not the case that the ostrich when going at full speed lowers its head or extends its wings. It rather raises its head to the fullest height, confirming the Scripture statement in the Book of Job (xxxix., 18), "What time she lifteth up herself on high, she scorneth the horse and his rider." In the spring you generally see in every estanzia a lot of their eggs, that have been brought in from the camp. The inhabitants use them to make omelets with, and chop them up with a salad; but they have a strong meaty flavour, which I thought sickening. The male bird sits on the eggs and hatches them, performing the office of nurse; while the female is released from nursery cares until the brood are able to walk forth with her. Verily ladies at home have too often an easy life of it compared to their lord and *master*, who is the worker and the bread-winner. If you approach the nest, the bird rushes out at the horse, spreading its wings, at which the horse is much alarmed.

An American colonel whom I knew tried the experiment of bolaing an ostrich for the first time on a fine horse that he had, and getting within the approved distance, just as he was intent on casting the bola, the ostrich made a double in a moment, like a hare, at right angles. The horse, which seemed better up to this movement than its rider, instantly did the same, and my friend and his bola were sent flying over the horse's head.

A very curious sight I have often seen is the marking cattle, which is done once every year. A large number are driven into an enclosure perfectly wild. The yearlings are selected first, and then the old bulls. One set of men attend to the fires in two or three places, keeping the iron estanzia marks hot,—such a mark as this

The horse peons and foot peons take their respective

stations. A man on horseback approaches the cattle to lasso one of the bulls, which crowd together in a corner and rush about. Having selected one, he throws his lasso round its head and horns, and the horse hauls it out of the throng. It rushes to some distance sideways. The sagacious and watchful horse, observing its movements, brings it up sharply when it has bolted to the end of its tether, and it rolls over and over again. It then tries the same experiment in an opposite direction, and with the same result. It roars, plunges, jumps, and resists to the utmost; and while doing this a foot peon throws his lasso, close along the ground, under its hind legs, drawing it tight, which disables it, and it falls to the ground on its side. A peon rushes to its head, which he keeps down by pressing its horn into the ground. Another peon at the fire, ready with one of the hot iron marks, runs out with it and presses the iron on its flank, which they say does not hurt the animal so much if it is red hot; smoke arises, and the ceremony is finished by removing the lasso from the horns.

If the animal to be marked is a full-grown bull, and perhaps a fierce one, a single horse may not be able to haul it out from the herd; in which case another peon on horseback casts a lasso under one of its hind legs and draws it tight while the bull is jumping, and he then hauls it in an opposite direction; so that one horse is pulling the bull by the horns in one direction, and the other by a leg in the contrary. While the bull is thus on its balance, a man pushes it on its side, and it falls to the ground, and is secured and branded as before. The next thing is to release the lassos, which is done first

to the one round its head; the other will drop down
on the ground as the bull moves. Up gets the bull in
a furious rage at the indignity practised upon him; and
will rush at the man on horseback, who rides among
the other cattle, which induces the bull to join them.
This business is all done regularly and like machine work,
till the whole herd is marked successively and successfully.
Perhaps, at the conclusion, there may be one bull or cow
lying with a broken neck, the result of the violent rushes
it has made. On some occasions all the men have to
" clear out " from the bull, by scrambling over the walls
of the enclosure.

I once came upon a striking scene in galloping across
camp: shall I say a scene of family grief? It was the
death of an old mare. I saw the mare lying on the
ground in the act of dying, and four of what seemed
to have been her colts and offspring in succession were
standing over her in a row, watching her. They looked
at me as I came near, and then down at the old
dying mare, who was evidently their mother, with every
imaginable sign of grief. One would now raise its
head, and then another, looking at me with a compassionate look, as much as to say, "Can you not
help us?" (I believe in the language of birds and
animals.) I approached quite close to them, and they
never moved, but stood over her, side by side, evidently in grief, watching her expiring. She was unable
to raise her head, but merely turned her eye towards
me, breathing very slowly. Slightly unmanned, I turned
and galloped away, reflecting on the mystery of suffering
from which even the brute beast is not exempt, but like

"the whole creation, groaneth and travaileth in pain together with us." A more touching episode of animal grief I never witnessed, associated as it was with the wildness of the desert scene; and I mused for the next hour and a half on the "spirit of a beast" "going downwards," as Solomon says (Eccles. iii., 12), and "man's upwards," vainly attempting to reconcile the mystery of animal life and death. Suddenly an ostrich started up in front of me, running before me for a mile, supposing I was chasing it; and instead of turning to one side, it kept in my line of gallop, a teru teru dipping at it and screaming, while the ostrich lowered its head and shook out its wings and feathers as the teasing bird pounced at it.

I thought what waste and prodigality of animal life there is in these vast wilds, where creatures, "like flowers that bloom, and waste their sweetness on the desert air," are born to live and die merely as *fruges consumere nati*, and that the earth should be replenished, and race repeated after race, to pass a useless and harmless existence, and then to return to its native earth again. God is doubtless glorified in these as in His other works, but to us they seem meanwhile profitless, until the desert is reclaimed, both literally and morally, and blossoms again like the rose.

In an open country like this, attention to tracks, whether of wheels or of horses, will soon enable you to follow correctly for many leagues any party in advance, especially as, from the absence of horse-shoes, there is no possibility of having them reversed to conceal the direction, as has been narrated in a case of robbing in England.

Not that you can ever pretend to come up to the tracking powers of either the Arab or the North American Indian.

An Arab, from inspecting the footsteps upon the sand, can tell, from the faintness or depth of the impressions, whether the person carried a load or not; whether he passed the same day or several days before. The unequal intervals between the steps show him whether he was fatigued or not; and from this he calculates the chance of overtaking him. And he can track a stolen camel to the very home of the thief, for several days' journey, no matter how many footsteps may have crossed the track in different directions; so that an offender can scarcely hope ever to escape detection in his clandestine proceedings.

In like manner the Northern Indian can read impressions upon the grass. He has his venison stolen. Taking his observations, he sets off in pursuit of the thief, tracking him through the woods. Meeting somebody, he asks if they have seen a little old white man with a short gun, accompanied by a small dog with a bob tail.

He judges the description thus:—"He must have been a little man, because he piled up stones to stand upon to reach the venison. He was old, because he took short steps, which the tracks upon the leaves showed. He was a white man, because he turned out his toes, which an Indian never does. His gun was a short one, from the mark that it made upon a tree against which it leaned; and his dog was a small one by its track; and it had a bob-tail, from the mark that it made in the dust where it sat while its master was stealing the meat."

So if a native in this country loses a cow, which another finds bogged, and takes the hide off, the owner is sure to be able to follow up the tracks made by the thief, and eventually discover and claim his property.

CHAPTER VIII.

Estanzia Houses—Poestas — Intercourse with Natives — Burial Custom — Marriages — Meat — Native Dining — Fuel — Mining Prospects—Sporting Places—Animals—Jaguar—Gatteo Montanos —Capincho—Visits to them—Glyptodon—Comadraka.

ALL the houses in this country are of the Spanish-Moorish sort, being with single rooms on a ground floor, one storey high, with flat tiled roofs, called an " azotea," on which you can walk. The rain runs from this into a rain-water well, called an " alheva," which stands by itself in the front or back of the house, and is surrounded with a low brick wall, leaving the aperture three or four feet in diameter. From this wall rises two brick or wooden pillars, with a little bridge across, from which is suspended a pulley, over which runs the rope to draw the bucket up out of the well. The poestas have hip roofs like our cottages, covered with sheet iron or a thatch of reed. The estanzia houses, which may be called the squire's residence, have generally one room on each side of the entrance, with windows on opposite walls, looking east and west. These rooms are lofty, and are barred from top to bottom. Even in the cities, from thieves abounding there, the windows are all barred; and you see the children inside these bars as you pass, which gives the appearance of their being imprisoned. Across the end of these rooms, that run from north to south, there are

three other rooms that are bed rooms, running east and
west, and projecting on each side of the others. The
spaces between these end rooms at the north and south
are enclosed overhead with either an azotea or with
a verandah roof. There are also large blinds, that draw
down in front of these verandahs during the heat of the
day; so that in the morning the family close the shutters
and windows on the east side of the house and sit out under
the verandah on the west side; and they reverse this order
in the afternoon, when the sun comes round to the west.

In your intercourse with the natives, certain things must
be carefully observed, to avoid giving offence. You must
never call a native a "Gaucho" (pronounced Gowcher),
which implies a wild savage; nor call a woman, a "Chino,"
or half-bred (equivalent to our female dog), as either would be
esteemed a term of reproach. If you call at a native's house,
and he offers you the customary "Matey," it is an offence to
decline it; though I always avoided taking it, thinking it unpleasant. Matey is a native beverage, which the women
especially are sucking all day long with a silver pipe,
out of a small sort of wooden pear that grows in the
country. If, in travelling, you are obliged to pass through
a widely extended flock of sheep, you must always *walk*
your horse through them, or it would cause the whole
flock to run together, which they are accustomed to do
every evening, when ridden up home; and you might
also divide a flock by so doing, and cause part of them
to go astray to a distance. As civility costs nothing,
"Mucho, mucho gratias," which sounds like dog Latin,
but is true Spanish here, will be considered friendly and
polite for any attention you receive.

When any one dies, he is put into a deal box, which is then placed on some of the low rocks that abound everywhere, with a small cross of two sticks stuck up above it, which every one understands the meaning of. This cross is never omitted in any place where a person has died, either by a violent death or otherwise, as in the tree in the sketch of the Pass of the Tichinango River.

The body remains in this state for some months, when the small wild animals and the weather will have caused nothing to remain but the bones. These are then put into a smaller box, on a horse; and, if a bone is too long to go into the box, it is stamped upon and broken shorter; and the box is sent off on horseback for burial, perhaps fifty miles off, to a Romanist burial ground.

No marriage is legal in this country (and, consequently, is not considered legal in ours,) but a Roman Catholic one, because that is the only religion recognised by the Government. If a Protestant desires to marry a Roman Catholic, every means is used by the priest in the town, to whom they have to go, and every impediment is applied, to induce the one to renounce Protestantism. The fees for marriage, as charged by the priest, are enormous—fifty dollars, or £10 English. Consequently, the great majority of couples live unmarried, in concubinage; which, however, is strictly honoured and respected. It is remarkable that this identical sum is demanded, and generally exacted, in Spain and Ireland, by the Romish priesthood. If two English persons wish to be married—no marriage by an English clergyman being legal, either there or at home, except by our English consular chaplains or naval chaplains

of the guardships—the parties are obliged, at great
expense, to go to Monte Video or Buenos Ayres, where
alone these are to be found. The Government have been
applied to on behalf of the English settlers, to legalise
a marriage by any English clergyman living in the camp.
They have refused to sanction this object, but have
partly promised to pass a civil act to legalize it as a
civil contract.

The meat that you get here is always that which has been
recently killed, which is unavoidable in warm countries, from
its not keeping many hours. At eight o'clock in the morning, you see a peon haul a sheep, by a rope round its neck,
to a post, plunge his long knife into the side of its neck,
and force it out edgeways in front, and, in half an
hour, you have some of it hot for breakfast. Mutton
thus killed is so excessively tough that it leaves us nothing
to do for some time but to chew it in silence, which is
anything but convivial.

No meat is ever hung, even in cold weather, when it
might be, for a couple of days, in which case it would
be tender. But it is contrary to the custom of the
country. All the meat that is cooked is never kept
and served up cold; for, in this state, no peon would
ever touch it; it would be considered an insult to any
native to offer it to him. So that it is all thrown to the
dogs. Every flock has a certain per-centage of capones or
wethers, for daily family use. In hot climates, more meat
is required to support the body. The general diet is
mutton and biscuits, and potatoes and vegetables, where
there is a keenta, or garden. American stoves are used in
the kitchens. The natives roast meat in the open air,

on an " assador." This is a piece of pointed iron stuck slanting in the ground, with a hook on the top, on which the meat is hung, and a fire is kindled between three stones placed on the ground underneath. This is called an " assou on an assador." The meat, being slightly smoked by this process, has really a better taste than on a spit before one of our fires. But what is thought best of all is " Carne con cuero," or flesh roasted with the skin on, in this manner; as the skin retains all the gravy in the meat. You see natives, especially in shearing time, hold up a long piece of meat with their left hand, seize the other end of it with their mouth, and cut it off with their knife close to their lips, and so on until it is finished.

The maize, when ground as farina, makes a good nourishing sort of poultice-pudding, depending on the condiments, and it is usually eaten with a jam made of preserved quinces, or of the peaches of the country. You get a good wine, called " Carlon," from Spain, costing, by the cask, ninepence per bottle. It is something in taste between Port, Claret, and Rousillon, and of the same dark colour.

The only fuel is wood, from the montes or woods that grow only by the side of the rivers. Among some nations in Mid-Africa, a bag is suspended under the tail of a horse, to catch the dung it may drop, which serves for fuel, on halting for the night; and so here the dung of sheep is very useful for this purpose. From so many sheep lying in the coral every night—the time when most is dropped—it will accumulate to a foot thick in a year; and, from being constantly trodden down, it is closely compressed. When a hot sun has been on it for a time, it is easily broken up into large lumps; and, if this is stowed away in a dry place, it becomes an excellent substitute for fuel, and burns with a strong glowing heat.

People living in this country are impressed with the idea that gold may be found here. The rocks are disintegrated granite, and quartz and mica are mixed with them. The proof can hardly be arrived at by merely examining the *débris* at the bottom of the streams; but it is necessary to go down to the original bed of the rivers, and penetrate through all more recent accumulations; for, if gold is there, this is the only place where it can be found. Australian diggers have assured me that, from the appearance, there can be little doubt but that gold can be found here.

In Brazil, gold-digging is given up for diamond-hunting. Both this jewel and mineral are found in great abundance in the neighbourhood of the San Francisco River, that runs for 1500 miles from the western side of the Organ Mountains, at Rio, and empties itself into the ocean between Bahia and Pernambuco. I question much whether this jewel may not be found among the rocky slopes and beds of rivers in this country. A writer on Brazil says of that country what may, perhaps, apply to this, "From rash mining speculations that have existed, a false conviction has resulted in Europe, that the seed of capital cannot be profitably sown in Brazil. But there is no country where, properly husbanded, it will bear a better crop."

As regards sporting, the Rio-Negro, and still more the Parana and Paraguay rivers, that is to say the woods upon their banks—to say nothing of the great interior towards the North, up to the confluents of the Amazon country, which is the least known of any part of the world—abound with unlimited wild sport. Many of the animals indigenous to these parts are exceptional with regard to other parts of the world.

As regards animals, the jaguar is extinct in Bánda Oriental, except in the Northern parts. Jaguar signifies "devourer of us," or man-eater. The puma, or South American lion, is found in the secluded woods by the sides of rivers. If they do not make themselves known by an extensive destruction of sheep, the floods generally drive them out, and they are soon shot. Several sorts of leopard cat, called Gatteo Montanos, are still very common. Some are just like leopards, as big as a good-sized dog, with black spots on a pale yellow ground. One killed near where I resided was 45 inches long from the nose to the end of the tail, though I have heard of their being 20 inches longer. Others are like a tabby cat, only with black spots instead of stripes. Others are yellow, with neither spots nor stripes, and with shaggy hair, very like that of the lynx.

The large rivers to the North West have many jaguars in them, which do not hesitate to attack men, and to swim the rivers in order to get at them. It is the most fierce and powerful of the feline tribe in this Continent, and is larger than the East Indian panther and leopard. During the great floods many are floated down the Parana and Paraguay rivers on large trees, which attack everything they meet when they get to shore. The specimen of the jaguar tribe in the den in the Zoological Gardens, adjoining the cage of the Bengal tiger, shows it to be next in size to that animal.

In Paraguay I was told that there are black leopards, with red spots, and eagles of a pink colour. The two largest eagles I ever saw, which are as big as condors, are now in the museum at Buenos Ayres, and were brought from the Paraguan country, which is so productive of wild animals.

The most remarkable animal, and which is peculiar to South America alone, is the capincho. It is called Capivara, from capim, the Brazilian word for green meat, as signifying the grass-eater; or capivara, in Indian; but capincho, in Spanish, for the water-hog. Its peculiarity consists in this, that though amphibious, like the tapir, and possessing the power of remaining under water,

CAPINCHO, OR CAPYVARÁ, OR WATER HOG.

it has not, like the tapir, a skin resembling the hippopotamus, but is furnished with long hair, and has no tail.

I was staying in the Macciel Camp, where these animals abound, and I frequently walked by the river for some hours, and thus had a fair opportunity of examining these curious animals in their living state. I came on five of them suddenly over a bank. Two of them dashed into the water, and two others prepared to do the same; the fifth, which was evidently an old male, gave a coughing bark, and stood still, without seeming afraid. Knowing it is the human eye that frightens animals I looked away, and walked slowly to one side, that the capincho might not be alarmed. It was the size of a large sheep, with long, coarse, rusty brown hair, fading to a flax colour under the neck and belly.

The animal has four toes on the front feet and three on the hinder, and they are partly webbed. The claws are thick at the base and pointed, approximating in shape to the hoofs of the pachydermata. Its mouth was remarkably coarse, and out of all proportion to the rest of the body; and it is very deep at the nose, having two long incisor front teeth in each jaw, like a rabbit. It seemed to be perfectly at home in the water, could continue in it for a long time without coming to the surface, and could walk on the bottom. The skin is used for making riding boots, but it will not stand wet. It is of a mottled reddish colour.

On another occasion, when walking near the river, I saw five capinchos browsing, like sheep, on the river bank, and eleven of them on the opposite bank, and by going frequently among them, and by walking slowly from them if they barked, they at last showed no signs of fear, and went on eating, evidently supposing I was some animal like themselves. It gave me an excellent opportunity of watching their habits. They are harmless, inoffensive animals, and live on the tala, and other trees, but chiefly on grass. I cannot believe that they eat fish, being evidently rodents. In a tree, twelve feet from the ground, an eagle was sitting on its nest. I climbed up and looked into the nest. It contained two eggs, not quite the size of those of a goose. The bird wheeled round over the tree while I was doing this, and immediately after I left, it resumed its sitting on the nest.

In the museum at Buenos Ayres I saw a fine and unique specimen of the antediluvian animal, the glyptodon, together with its shell. It must have been very much akin to the capincho in its habits of life, from the formation of its jaws and feet. Dr. B——, the curator, kindly gave me a sketch of it that he had had printed. This antediluvian skeleton was found in the Buenos Ayres side of the Plate, which abounds in the finest specimens of the Megatherii of former worlds. It is from that country that our finest specimens in the British Museum came, though not exclusively so. It must have been of great strength, and about the size of the hippopotamus, from the massive bones of the hind legs and tail. It probably had been accustomed to stand upon its hind legs, supporting itself by its tail, like the kangaroo, and drawing down branches and tearing up roots with its fore legs, which are much smaller. It was clearly a rodent, and, from the formation of the bones of its feet, its habits must have been similar to the capincho. If so, it presents a curious agreement between an extinct antediluvian animal, and one of the present time. Its massive shell, 3 inches thick, and mammulated, had no scales upon it like the armadillo's that exist here now. I saw bones of this animal that were found in the bed of a river on the North side of the Plate.

The comadraka abounds here. It is strictly an opossum, having a pouch for its young ones, which they scramble in and out of, in case of danger. It lives in holes in the ground. The body is black, with a white stripe on the sides. The end of the tail, for six inches, is free from hair, and of a yellow colour, and it is prehensile. It feeds on flesh, and is fond of poultry, and for this reason it is destroyed wherever it is found. At a poesta that had not been occupied for some time, in the holes around it, during the first eight months, no less than fifty of these animals were killed, besides thirty skunks. The feet on each leg are like the human hand, whereas the skunk has toes, with long, sharp claws, not much unlike those of a bird, and it is very different to the English one. The natives eat the flesh of the legato, and the armadillo is considered of excellent flavour, though I never experimented upon either.

CHAPTER IX.

Variety of Birds—Querables—Anecdote of Sheep Coral and Querables—Horn-winged Birds—Teru—Widow and Scissor Birds Hawks—Everything Destructive—Fishes—Lobo—Snakes—Bite of and Cure—Spider—Its Bite—Religious View of the People—Ignorance Under Popery—Opportunity for Converting Them—No Hindrances—False Principles of Romanism—Inquiry Awakened—Expectations Excited—Contrast with Romanism on West Coast—Degraded Moral State of Brazil.

THERE is a beautiful variety of birds of every class to be found here. The eagles are of three sorts. But the common scavenger of the country is the querable, a black bird, about the size of a raven, only that it has a crooked beak. Everything is tame in this country because it is never molested, and the natives have seldom guns, and never powder. There is a wild spot which I used to visit, where two rivers meet, with large boulders of rocks piled up naturally; and I have sat on the top of them with five-and-twenty of these vultures wheeling round close over my head, besides a dozen eagles higher, and perfectly fearless of me. These querables are common, and familiar everywhere, and when brought up tame, they will follow you on horseback for leagues into the camp, and eat meat out of your hand.

I was staying at one estanzia where the sheep coral joined the house, and contained at night 2700 sheep. Now a flock ought never to consist of more than 1000, or 1200, because, if a lamb becomes separated from its mother, it has no chance of ever finding her again in such a multitude. The consequence is that it gets faint and lies down; and when very young it will soon die if neglected. The morning after I arrived at this house I went out into the coral. There were 110 of these black vultures and 10 coranchio hawks sitting on the hurdles around it in a row. Six expiring lambs, besides many that had been devoured, were lying about, with four vultures on each, picking the eyes and kidneys out of the lambs before they were quite dead.

I walked sideways near these birds and they would hardly move; some of them hopped off, but they soon hopped on again, and went on eating. I walked round inside this coral within four yards of these vultures, and they never offered to fly away. I thought this was a singular specimen of bad farming; for had the flock been divided, all these lambs, and there were many, could have been saved. I never saw the like of this in any part of the camp that I visited. The only excuse alleged—on my expostulating for allowing such pests to exist—was, that one day twenty-five of these birds had been killed, but the following day 200 fresh ones came.

There are an abundance of cranes of different sorts. Some large birds of snowy whiteness, with black backs, and standing upwards of four feet high, are very common. If you are on foot they are shy, from having been shot at; but on horseback you may ride among them without their hardly moving. One peculiarity that runs through several tribes of birds that are not of the hawk tribe— from the largest to those not bigger than a thrush—is,

that they are horn-winged, as their means of defence.
I shot a very fine specimen of the "Yok-haus," which
is a sort of wild turkey, with a powerful beak, and is the
largest of the horn-winged class.   It was about twelve
pounds in weight and six and a half feet across the
wings; and it had a three-sided horn like a bayonet,
three inches long, on the centre joint of the wing, and
a shorter one at the next outer joint.   When the wings
are shut these horns lay across the breast in the front.
The bird, when shot, was in the act of eating alfalfa or
lucerne, though it also eats flesh.

The teru teru, or horn-winged plover, is common everywhere.   Generally two or three pairs of them are located
round each poesta.   It is a very watchful bird, and gives
an alarm in the darkest night in tones which a native can
understand to mean that a horse, a dog, a cow, or a
person are passing.   This is a perennial inhabitant of the
camp.

There is a variety of the plover and other kinds of
birds which come, and seem to replace each other, at
certain months of the year.   These latter afford excellent
sport, and are good eating, which the teru is not.   That
bird is so called from its note, which it repeats twice.
In places that are overflowed in winter, the snipe, teal,
and wild ducks cover the moist places, and are delicious
eating.

A long-necked partridge, that pipes and lays black
eggs, is common everywhere, which you can knock over
with a pebble or a catapult.   They always disclose their
presence in the long grass by beginning to pipe.   Their
flesh is white, stringy, and tasteless, and not fit for the

table, even when kept a few days. "The large partridge," the size of a duck, is much better. These birds being unable to fly long or far, are chased on horseback with dogs. The bird flies first 150 yards; when put up a second time, about eighty; and a third time, thirty; and is then easily run into by the dogs.

A great variety of birds like woodpeckers are to be seen, of varied and bright plumage; and green parrots. The latter build a nest, about six feet high and four across, in the poplar trees, full of holes, like a dovecote, each hole being for one pair of birds. The most singular bird that arrives here early in the summer is the scissor bird, of the size and colour of a swallow, only that it has a tail a foot long that shakes as it flies behind it, like a long black ribbon, and when the bird flies round the tail opens like a scissor. The ornaro, or oven bird, builds its nest of black mud, like a Hottentot's hut, in two compartments, in every direction about the camp and houses, and generally on the top of a post. And there is a little bird called the widow bird, snowy white, with wattle round its eyes; and it is always accompanied by another, half black and half white, which we will suppose to be the widower.

The hawk tribe are of splendid plumage. I came twice on a magnificent pair, and rode close round them. They were very large, and of a brilliant yellow colour, and speckled with brown on the coverts and back, with yellow crests from the back to the front of the head, with a black edge. The natives will ride round a bird, gradually approaching nearer, and so confuse it, that, with a long stick, they can slip a noose over its head. You can buy the prepared skins of birds in Rio at from 20–50 shillings a hundred, so that this is a fine field for the bird-stuffer and the entomologist.

In the camp you will come upon a flock of birds like our blackbirds, only with breasts of a fiery red. Farther on you will meet with another such a flock, only with breasts of a bright yellow. So refulgent are the former in the sun, that they each look like a flame of fire. There is also a little bird red all over, that, when the sun shines upon it, looks as if it were on fire.

There is one rule with all creatures in this country —insects, birds, and beasts—and that is, that the nearer the equator, the larger they are, and their qualities, whatever they may be, are the stronger. As everything here is savage and cruel, so do the rivers abound with fish of the most destructive powers. The piranha is about a foot and a half long. They say that a shoal of them will, in ten minutes, reduce a bullock to a skeleton, in the water. A fish, two and a half feet long, with sharp teeth, is found in the rivers, that will attack a man bathing. I knew a gentleman who was laid up six weeks, from being seized by the leg by one of them, as he was coming out of the water.

In small pools, you can catch fish of 4–6 pounds weight, and in small rivers of 18 or 20 pounds. There is also a dangerous animal to meet with in the waters, called the Lobo, something between an otter and a seal, which will readily attack you. I saw three swimming fearlessly near me, with a very threatening aspect. Even the little fish, three inches long, have teeth out of all proportion to their size.

So far, I have mentioned the agreeables of a camp life;

but, I must also state some of the disagreables, and these
are insects and snakes.

The coral snake is exceedingly handsome, with scarlet
and cream-coloured marks, in alternate squares. The bite
is very deadly, as they say—fatal in a quarter of an hour.
According as travellers have experienced instances of this
at different seasons of the year, they will either allow or
deny this point. One thing is certain, namely, that the
bite of both serpents and insects is more venomous in the
hottest weather than in the cold; and, as I mentioned
before, nearer the equator than farther from it. In the
hottest weather, I believe, as a rule, that if a man is bitten,
and applies no remedies, he will die from the bite. If he
is bitten in the face or the head, where you cannot
stop the poison communicating by a ligature, this is the
usual result. If he is bitten in the hand or leg, a
tight bandage should be immediately applied above the
part, to intercept, as much as possible, the poison from
going to the heart. The bite should be cut out, am-
monia rubbed in, and a tea-spoonful taken internally;
or, if none is at hand, the bite should be burnt with a
lucifer match.

The police, at their stations in India, are always furnished
with antidotes of this kind. The action of the poison is
to stop the movement of the heart; and, after death from
it, it is found that the blood will never congeal, but
remains always liquid. To keep up the action of the
heart, is, therefore, the first thing to be attended to.
The man must be compelled to keep moving about. I
have even known a man tied behind a gig, and compelled to run. He must take a pint of cannia, or other

F

spirit, and repeat it; and, if he becomes drunk under this, he will recover; if not, he will die.

The bite of the spider is sometimes fatal in hot weather. You can hardly walk in any part of the camp for fear of stepping on these insects. There is the tarantula, a reddish-black hairy spider, about three inches long in the body, beside the legs; and the green crab spider, which is without hair, and has a hard shell like a crab; and if it is touched with a stick, it will stand up stiff, and ready to strike with its forceps and feet. I have met a dozen of these odious things in one day in my walks. I knew a peon whose ankle was stung by a spider, and a large bladder arose holding about a pint of liquid, and when it broke, he felt no ill effects from it; but he was a strong man. A boy twelve years old was bitten at the bottom of his back, under his clothes, by a small black spider, and died from it. The medical men pronounced that he was poisoned by it. Scorpions and centipedes and the coral snake are more apt to come into the house than the tarantula. There are black snakes, two yards long, of which I saw many, but they are harmless. I heard of a boa, thirteen feet long, which had been seen among rocks in a certain place three springs following (in October), which is the time when, after hybernation, these reptiles show themselves freely in the day time. I was, however, prevented, by returning home, from seeing it alive in its natural state. The small stag, which you often meet with here, has a method of killing snakes by jumping over them and descending with all four feet upon them, and bounding off.

The usual and eccentric mode of publicly demonstrating

Sabbath joy here is by letting off, at the Government expense, rockets and fireworks on a Sunday afternoon or evening.

The condition of the natives of all this country, in a religious point of view, is just as we might expect from their utter ignorance of Bible knowledge and of revealed truth. No nation left to its own resources has ever become civilized. The Indian of one century is found to be the Indian of other centuries, with the same weapons, the same habits, observances, and vices; and some nations have, in the course of time, become even more degraded than their ancestors were. Where civilization has progressed, the cause of this has to be referred to the knowledge derived from intercourse with civilized nations. But you find that the source of *their* education in turn has been from a God-serving people, to whom revealed religion has been committed. As regards polished manners, civilization has done much for the nations of South America; but religion has done nothing. In this respect they are in a pitiable state of ignorance. It has been the policy of the Jesuit priesthood of the past day, and of the Romish priesthood of the present, to leave and keep these people in utter religious ignorance, under the assumed idea that ignorance is the parent of devotion, but in reality that no inquiry may be made into the false creed of an apostate Church.

But here I must in fairness draw a contrast with this state of things in the south-eastern cities, and the religious feeling shown in the Roman Catholic cities of the West Coast of America, favourable to the latter. Here you never see the piety that makes every one stop, in the very act of what they are doing, the moment they hear the evening bell for the oracion, or prayer—no matter how distant it may be—in Lima and Peru. The traveller stops and joins in the devotion, dictated by the distant hum of that bell that floats on the air. The workman, in the very act of digging, stands motionless as a statue at the work he is engaged in; the horse is instantly brought to a standstill; and nature itself seems hushed for a few moments, that it may join in a prayer of adoration to the common Creator of all.

No man can deny that this is a striking and pleasing act of devotion, as distinct from the fact that it proceeds from a religion with which we cannot coincide. But if it proceeds forth as the outpouring of even a false religion, as a public attestation to the honour and power of Him " in whom we all live and have our being;" can we boast of as much in our Protestant England? Where shall we find in our country, at the sound of our church bells, any such outward acknowledgment of God as is so daily shown by Mahometans, at sunrise, sunset, and at their meals?

It seems extraordinary that our great societies—the Gospel Propagation Society and the Church Missionary Society—should never have made any attempt to send missionaries and Bibles into any of these parts of South America. It was not until some few years ago, when a gentleman, named Gardiner, went to the extreme south of the continent, and perished from starvation while in the attempt to convert the natives, that public attention seemed drawn to the need of missionary work in this vast continent. Struck with the noble and self-sacrificing spirit of this first missionary, a society was formed in Bristol, which afterwards expanded into the South American Missionary Society, and removed to London, and which for some years has sent missionaries and chaplains, who now occupy stations, not merely around the coast of South America, but in many places in the interior. Their work is successful and progressing; and the Word of God is brought home to our isolated countrymen in many of the secluded spots and settlements where they have affixed their abode.

South American nations now present a more hopeful appearance, in a religious point of view, than did the nations of antiquity when the Gospel was first offered to them. They may now be likened to a field that has been lying fallow for many years, ready to receive the seed sown, and to produce a plentiful harvest, when God, in His providence, shall decree that the cloud now resting upon them shall be dispelled, and that light shall be shed abroad over these dark lands.

Here there is no hindrance to the work of spreading Gospel knowledge among these nations. In India we have to encounter the subtle Buddhist and the intellectual Mahometan. In Europe we have to contend with the many-headed hydra of political nonconformity, and the hard materialist unbelief of the rationalist. But no such mighty opponents and hindrances exist here. The people —particularly in the wide expanse of the camp, where they have little communication with each other — are without any religion; for they are only nominally Roman Catholics. Romanism is, to all intents and purposes, *effete* and worn out in the camp. The liberal institutions of these free Republics ensure a ready access to the people for missionary efforts. Therefore, as the door is open, now is the time to avail ourselves of the opportunity for effecting the conversion of the people.

The religion of Romanism being the offering of the solitary mass by the priest as a propitiation for the sins of the living and the dead, in which act you need take no part, as the priest can do all for you, and you may remain passive in your sins; the natural consequence is, that no personal religion is ever produced under such a system as this. Men are severed from the performance of duties under the system of the priest being alone answerable for souls, and as being himself the only means of access to heaven.

Such being the case, the priests in the towns occupy themselves in nothing else but in sacrificing mass, which is considered sufficient; and therefore they never travel into the camp, to visit and instruct the native inhabitants. In fact the distances are so great, that, in addition to their usual occupation, it would hardly be possible for them to do so. I have reason to think that in the western cities of South America the Romish priesthood and Governments are more illiberal, more actively hostile to Protestantism, and more persecuting by far than in cities on the east coast, where the civil institutions are more liberal, Popery more listless and indifferent, and no proselytising going on.

From newspapers carried into the camp, which the Spanish native reads, the tidings of what is going on in Spain, the religious freedom that has there begun, and the knowledge of religious truth that is there spreading, has deeply interested this people. They now desire to have the same communicated to themselves. A doubt is suggested as to the truth of Popery, and a consequent spirit of inquiry has arisen. Every Spanish Gospel and tract is eagerly received and read; and a strong wish for religious instruction prevails just in proportion as these things are in operation. In short, with respect to the existing desire for it, no place presents a more inviting field for missionary exertions than South America. What is wanted is a Spanish-speaking missionary to go amongst the people, or a reader, to preach and explain the Gospel to them.

A gentleman who travelled in Brazil in 1860 says, speaking of that country, "All men have full and entire liberty to profess any religion they choose, and to worship God as they like, save only that their places of worship must not be in the form of a temple or church." This has been judicially decided to mean only that they may not build steeples or ring bells.

The Church here is altogether dependent on the civil government. The emperor is chief of the executive power, and exercises it by his ministers of state. Their powers are, among others, to nominate the bishops and to provide for their ecclesiastical support. No bishop can confer orders without special licence of the emperor; and neither bishops nor priests can leave their dioceses or parishes without a special permit from the Government. The civil power is invariably exerted on the side of toleration, and offers a constant and steady opposition to all bigotry. There is great ignorance, immorality, and corruption prevailing among the Brazilian priesthood.

Many of them never pretend to officiate. Preaching is not recognised as part of the weekly services of the Church, except by one or two metropolitan padres, who record some hideous deeds of St. George and the Dragon, &c., &c., in one or two feast-days of the year. The ignorance and sloth of the clergy seem almost incredible. Many priests are hardly able to read the service. No such thing as parochial visitation is ever heard of. Almost universal immorality prevails throughout the land among the clergy, who are more debased than other classes; so that no one will trouble himself to go to confess to a padre whose morality is inferior to his own. Every year the official reports of the Minister of Justice and the provincial residents complain of this. And what are the usual customs? Sunday is hardly observed at all. In Rio the shops are open, and the people amuse themselves as they like. Military parades are commonly held on that day; and operas, theatres, and balls are more crowded than usual. Only a short time ago it was the regular day for auctions.

And what is the natural result of all this? The Brazilians themselves laugh while they conform to such worship, and bow before such saints and images as are there. Indeed, nearly all public worship is performed by women, who mumble over their beads in the intervals of the levities they carry on in church, and whose presence alone attracts the sterner sex there. Religion, as a principle operative on individual and social life, is, to all appearance, extinct in Brazil. The outward form of Romanism is there universally acknowledged, and as generally laughed at. The spirit and power of Christianity may be said to be unknown. It is quite sufficient with the people to excuse any error by saying, "I am a bad Catholic." All this shows how feeble is the hold that the Roman Catholic faith has on the Brazilian mind, and how ready the country is for the reception of a better knowledge of a purer faith.

CHAPTER X.

I now come to speak, in my concluding sketches of this interesting country, of the seasons, and especially of the stormy and unusual times that occurred during the year 1868. That year was so entirely different to previous and usual years as to weather, that, by pointing out its exceptional character, we can more correctly show what the usual run of weather is here. The year 1868 may well be remembered as the earthquake year, and be called so, from the severity of the visitation; although there was no terrestrial disturbance in any part of the east coast of this continent. The dreadful earthquakes that took place on the west coast seemed to have spread their influence to this part in the shape of unusual atmospheric disturbances that quite altered the regular course of the seasons on this side of the country. Extraordinary rains, in fact, have always been the accompaniment of earthquakes. I was informed that, as a rule, in about every five years a "Seco" or drought, of more or less severity and continuance, happens here. It may be imagined what an effect and injury would be produced on a vast pastoral country from a visitation like this.

From the tenacious nature of the soil, it is enabled to retain a vast amount of moisture. It is said that rain is required to penetrate to a great many feet deep to enable the soil to sustain the grass in a protracted time of heat, to meet the great evaporation of moisture that takes place. Droughts have ever been a drawback to this country, though they by no means exist to the same extent as in Australia or at the Cape of Good Hope.

The ruin to stock generally follows this course:—The grass becomes entirely eaten down and has no power to grow, from the great heat and the absence of wet. When nothing remains above ground, the sheep scratch up the roots of the grass, and eat them. Last of all, they eat the Chilka, a poisonous weed that has a white flower, and in ten minutes they die. A flock soon disappears under this unpropitious weather. This is, in a measure, always the case when there is a preponderance of dry weather in the hot season ; so that the flocks suffer, while no actual seco or drought can be said to exist. But the year 1868 has been noted for quite the reverse to all this, and for a very great excess of rain beyond what is usual.

The heat begins in November and lasts until February. In March the weather gets cooler, with rain in May, and still more in June and July, excepting the "St. Iwan Summer," of a fortnight, when it seems to return to Midsummer heat again. July, August, and the beginning of September, being the depth of winter, are cool and wet months, when the rivers become flooded.

There is, properly, no wet weather here, as in England. The only rain is from thunderstorms—nature's mode of relieving itself of the great electricity that is in the air. "Temporals" return once a week or a fortnight, or oftener, and very severe these storms are. During this year, the storms have exceeded anything before known here, and evidently they must have been the effect of terrestrial convulsions at a distance. But, while these storms have been so frequent, there has been but little rain at Rio, 1100 miles to the north. And I found that at Bahia, 1800 miles to the north, they had been perfectly without rain for six months.

As the heat increases, from the early spring, the storms do also, in the violence of the lightning and thunder, and the weight of rain that falls. But, in this year, the storms followed each other in succession, with the intermission of about three days only. And I have known it to rain, in one continued down-pour, for twelve or fourteen hours.

In the depth of winter, a piercing "Pampero" wind (that is, one blowing from the Pampas) will pierce you through and through, much more than any wind in England. Your sensitiveness to this wind may probably arise from attenuation of blood, owing to the heat you have been exposed to. But the wind itself is different from ours. It is a *soft* cold wind, and, therefore, the more piercing. It is very probable that it is a wind that come from the soft Pacific, and gets cooled in passing over the snowy Andes range, thus causing it to have this property. At all events, you require abundance of thick clothing for the short time that this wind occurs. It is also often accompanied by a dense fog for some days, like a London November fog. The wind is never in puffs, but when it blows, both in summer and winter, it is one continued steady blow, for twenty to thirty hours together.

When the first indications of the earthquake took place, on the west coast, I was at Buenos Ayres. Returning in the evening, from dining in the suburbs, the whole atmosphere to the north seemed enveloped in thunderstorm. And, when only two quadras from my lodging, the "Temporal" came down in an instant; and, before I could put a mackintosh on, I was wet through. In this short distance I had to go through water nearly a foot deep, before I reached my destination. The next day I found that three people had been killed by lightning, thirty had been drowned in nine lighter boats, that were blown over; and several unfinished houses had been blown down. In the street where the storm first came on is a moveable foot-bridge, crossing from pavement to pavement. The next day I saw that the water that had passed down the street the night before was five and a half feet deep, from the straws that were adhering to the rails of the bridge.

In starting for long rides in such weather, in the camp, I had need to look out for squalls. On the 3rd of October, having to ride twenty-seven miles to the M— estanzia, to the north, though the day was bright, I saw a black line close down along the southern horizon, with a slight flicker of light about it. I knew we should have the storm before evening; but, having a powerful and fast horse, I thought that I could cover my ground before I was over-

taken by it. I accordingly rode four and a half leagues
northwards, towards the St. Iwan river, and halted twenty
minutes at the poesta of two young English gentlemen,
just commencing the al-fresco patriarchal life of sheep-
farming. Finding the storm rising behind me, with its
significant artillery, I had no time to lose; and, as the
river a mile off was much swollen, I had to go farther up
the side of it, to a higher pass. When I crossed it I had
seven miles further to go. A poesta was on the horizon,
about five miles off, and to reach it was my only chance of
shelter. I accordingly stood in my stirrups, put the horse
to racing pace, and, dashing across two small streams,
I, with difficulty, and plenty of whipping, reached within
150 yards of the poesta, when the tempest was on me in a
moment in torrents. The horse was inclined to stop and
turn; but, by dint of flogging, I reached shelter.

This poesta had an iron roof, under which, when the
rain beat, it was impossible to hear the voice. The occupant was a diminutive old Londoner—as I soon discovered, by his dislike to and avoidance of the eighth
letter of the alphabet when he spoke English—who had
been in the country twenty-seven years. Chatting with him,
I watched the deluge that was going on outside for an hour
and a half, and I never witnessed such a down-pour. The
atmosphere seemed to be as full of water as of air, so that
you could not see thirty yards for rain. At the expiration
of this time, the slopes of the plain looked as if they were
covered with snow, but it was the water rolling along.
There was a lull in the storm, though it was densely black
all round, with continued lightning shooting down on all
sides. As I had two miles to go, to reach the estanzia,

the old gentleman told me he thought I might do it if I could gallop it in less than ten minutes. I, therefore, saddled and galloped, through water from one to three feet deep at the slopes; and, when I ascended a rise, a mile off, I saw the M— estanzia; but there also seemed to be rain pouring down in a dense mass just beyond the house. So I again raced at the utmost speed the horse would go, dashed into the back yard of the house, tore off the saddle and my valise, and in a moment another such a torrent was repeated, and for the same length of time, as the one that I had just before escaped.

Such rain had never been witnessed before; the river I crossed rose twenty feet in a quarter of an hour. Near the mouth of the San Carlos river 1500 sheep were swept away from a corner of the camp. I measured the height the flood rose there, and found it was 35 feet perpendicular.

A young gentleman on a visit at this estanzia was not so fortunate. He had ridden out with his gun, and had shot an eagle and a fox that jumped up before him Returning to the house, he reached to within 400 yards of it, when, the storm commencing, his horse turned round and would not face it, as they generally do. And he was obliged to sit, with his gun, the eagle, and fox on his horse, for an hour and a half, under that pitiless and howling tempest, until it ceased.

It is stated by old captains of ships that no one can prognosticate or foresee what the weather will be in this country. And, to a person who is accustomed to think himself weather-wise, the rapidity with which storms arise is surpising; for they come without giving any indications of their approach.

I was once a mile and a half to the westward of a poesta that I used to frequent. It was a bright sunny day, with a stiff breeze blowing from the southward. I saw a small storm on the westward horizon, very distant, and, as I thought, surely going northward. I looked at it presently again, and saw it had attained considerable elevation. In ten minutes more, I saw it was wheeling round and coming rapidly in my direction, homewards to the east. I mounted my horse and galloped for home. This little cyclone seemed to be bearing down upon me, and it was on me before I could reach home by half a mile, when a flash descended on the ground 200 yards to my left. The old horse darted away like the wind, and I barely escaped a severe ducking.

In one of these great storms, a gentleman I know was travelling through the camp, and he saw in front of him two old bulls in mortal conflict, when a flash descended and laid them both dead. I knew a settler who had 230 sheep killed in his coral by one stroke of lightning. Were this place peopled like England, these storms would probably cause many deaths.

We seemed for a long time destined to have a repetition of these storms, with increasing violence. Towards evening the clouds would gather darkly round. The keenta would be brilliantly illuminated with the fire-flies suddenly exploding into flame and then going out—perhaps as a sort of love-making to their mates, as is alleged to be the practice of our glow-worm. Then the thunder would roll nearer from all sides, the rain begin to drop, and the fire-flies go to bed. It seemed to be a perfect battling of the elements from every quarter, disputing, as it were, what was to be the direction the wind should take, with the utmost violence. The forked lightning would descend in eight and ten places at a time without cessation. Sleep was out of the question, and the lightning was so vivid, that, if you kept your eyes open, you could see nothing after a flash.

For fourteen long hours one night I watched the eccentric variety of this proceeding. For a considerable time it seemed to be raining lightning, so numerous and repeated were the flashes. It would shoot along sideways and upwards, bursting in jets of forks down, or fiddling down in zig-zag streams. Then the thunder would give an awful bounce, a grind, like vast rocks grinding together with a roar; a thrumming, mumbling, and a violent shaking, that made the house, doors, and windows rattle from top to bottom. This was just at the time the earthquake occurred, of which these were some of the effects. It gave one an idea of what the bombardment of Sebastopol must have been like.

During one particular night, the lightning had the singular appearance, as it poured down, of being a bright violet colour, with pink edges. A memorandum I made, of the 21st of October, was " the north and south wind had a tremendous passage at arms last night, from nine o'clock until nine o'clock this morning, exchanging volleys of thunderbolts and batteries of thunder—such lightning as never was witnessed in this country."

On one occasion, I saw, about a mile off, a globe of fire, which burst, shedding down a cascade of forked lightnings, which appeared to split into several more, that twisted and twirled, and shot, some upwards and some to the horizon, and returned back again. This celestial curtain lecture, however, at length ended—as Socrates and his wife Zantippe did, and much in the same way, when she poured water upon him—namely in torrents of rain and hail. I measured the fall of rain in one of these severe nights, and it was just as much as falls in England in a twelvemonth, that is twenty-six inches. September always ends with a three-days' tempest, called Santa Rosa's, because occurring about that saint's day. But it lost its distinctiveness this year, in the many that prevailed in that month.

As a reason for the existence of so much more wind in the southern hemisphere of the earth than in the northern, the greater predominance of water over land has been given. So that in the extreme southern part of Terra del Fuego incessant gales blow in that latitude round the world, from west to east. This also will apply to the Cape of Good Hope. Hence so difficult is it for ships to sail westward round these extremities of the continents, that they always prefer availing themselves of the wind, by taking the eastern route home.

But this, I believe, is to be referred back to another cause than the amount of water, and that is the action of the moon on the tides, of which this may be the effect. One thing is clear, as a consequence of these winds, that in average years much less rain falls in these southern parts than in the northern hemisphere. " Secos," or extreme draughts, being periodical in the most southern parts of both these continents. When the wind is north, it brings great heat with it. If south, there are cooler breezes ; but, in addition, violent winds, pamperos, and temporals, with thunder and lightning.

There are certain periods when the earth seems to

require to be relieved by earthquakes and volcanic erup-
tions, from the pressure of increasing subterranean forces.
These, like everything else, have their use. There seems
to be a compensating equilibrium necessary to be constantly
preserved; so that it has been supposed that scarcely a
day passes without some volcanic vibration taking place,
though scarcely perceptible, in some part or other of the
earth's surface. But such destructive earthquakes as signal-
ized the year 1868 in South America have seldom occurred;
and none have taken place with such awful results, and
of such a wide extent, as in this year, since 1755, when
Lisbon was destroyed; or, perhaps, since the times of
Herculaneum and Pompeii.

Volcanoes seem to be the legitimate outlets for the
earth's internal humours, and to be appointed for that
purpose as a safety valve. While the earthquake may be considered to be as the more eccentric effort to accomplish this.

Of all places, the range of the Andes, for 1700 miles,
from north to south, on the west coast of America, and
especially central America—which is Mexico and Nicaragua—seem to have been, both in known and unknown
times, the great seat of the volcanic action of the earth.
While the Cordillera of the Andes contain forty either
active or extinct volcanoes, in central America, from
Panama northwards, there are numberless large or small
volcones, some of them rising a sheer 15,000 feet
from the plain. But all are situated on the coast of
the Pacific.

Scientific men have assigned to igneous and volcanic
action all the important changes that the world has
undergone. And it has been attempted to account for

the elevated belt of mountains that runs across Africa, from east to west, near the equator, by assigning, as a reason for the elevation of that region from 3000 to 8000 feet, that it is caused by the action of the earth in its orbit. The effect being, by the elevation of this region, that, though lying in the hottest latitude, the climate is comparatively mild. But, if centrifugal force, from the earth's revolution on its axis, is to account for the range of the mountains of the moon in Africa, this would be a contrary reason for the elevation of. the Andes range, running, as they do, from north to south, and that to a far higher elevation. In fact, no reason can be assigned as a cause for the volcanic·elevation of this part of the world any more than for the existence of volcanoes elsewhere.

We have no reason to think that the earth's internal forces are diminishing because philosophers, in examining indications, have mistaken a prolonged action during many centuries as the effect of one single outburst.

Nor, in a contrary point of view, are we to apprehend that these subterranean humours will, some day, acquire such power that they will destroy the earth at one blow. Either such a view is too materialistic to be for. a moment entertained. We must not leave out one important item in thinking on_ this subject, which is the power, the will, and the providence of the Almighty. We know, on Scripture authority as well as on scientific, that the world was once destroyed by water; and fire, it is predicted, shall hereafter be the instrument, as water once was. These are equally in the hands of Him who ordereth all things in heaven and earth, and under the earth. Science may conjecture probabilities, but it is for Scripture to reveal the

decree that the earth shall be burned up, and all that it
contains, and the elements shall melt with fervent heat.

One thing is certain. Though hereafter subterranean
agency may be employed as a destroying, and not as a cor-
recting, power, in past ages it has had its use. It has served
to store up for us materials largely contributing to our comfort. The coal we burn would never have been condensed
had not forests and swamps been for long sunk beneath the
ocean. The very stones of our houses have been com-
pacted together by the pressure of superincumbent *débris*.
Besides all this, the range of the Andes has its use in
tempering both the heat and the cold of sea and land
in parts that are far distant from them.

The almost continually living on horseback, that travelling in this country demands, makes you sometimes feel
like a worn-out old post-boy. And it reminds you of
those little ancient boys you remember to have seen in
days gone by; the antiquated remains of the time when
"ladies of quality" were accustomed to drive about in
" a glass coach."

But if a man really wishes to see the wild, the free,
and the savage parts of creation, he must never think
of sparing himself. Any one who travels here should
be able to bear heat and cold, hunger and thirst, and
fatigue, for eight hours' continual galloping. He should
be somewhat of an iron constitution, and certainly be
no epicure. Without seeking adventures, he must expect,
in his travels through these countries, to have his path
sometimes beset with dangers. And he should never
travel by himself, as I did for 4000 miles without a
companion; for if an accident were to happen to him,

his bones even might not be found in these vast un-peopled wilds. The ancients seem to have been aware of this; for, in the Book of Ecclesiastes, iv., 9 and 10, it is written, "Two are better than one;" "for if they fall, the one will lift up his fellow; but woe to him that is alone when he falleth; for he hath not another to help him up."

A gentleman told me he was travelling by himself through the camp, and his horse fell, from putting its leg into one of the deep holes in the camp; and he was thrown with violence to the ground, and his ankle injured so that he could not walk. The horse got away from him before he could recover himself, and he lay on the ground disabled for some hours, no habitation being within sight. At length he saw a native riding in the distance, and he made signs to him, and was rescued; although he had expected to have remained there until he perished from hunger. A sense of being disabled as well as lost is anything but pleasant in a wild desert place.

The traveller must be prepared to balance agreeables and disagreeables against each other, and to bear with many things that are distasteful and unendurable to English habits and feelings. The thought, however, of returning home,—the resigning the free open-air life of a traveller, without the restraints of collar and neck-tie, in a beautiful country and climate, where every one is friendly,—and the idea of resuming civilization, and to mind your p's and q's, in stifling rooms and damp fogs, and a smoky air at home, with artificial cares and slavish conventualisms, is like a sow washed returning to wallow in the mire again. At all events, the most refined and luxurious will gain the lesson that a man's worldly enjoyment does not consist in the mere habits of English home life, and that climate will make you acquainted with more real enjoyment than is to be found in society and habits that are customary at home.

Even to travellers in search of health, variety, or amusement, there is every inducement held out to bend their steps in this direction. No voyage you can make is in a calmer sea, after you have passed the English Channel and Biscay, than from England to South America. Here you are wafted along by an unvarying favourable trade wind from north to south, through climates both hot and mild, where every comfort and luxury attend you in the voyage, and where, when you arrive in the country, unbounded hospitality greets you wherever you go.

Incidents and occurrences in travelling here are strange, striking, and instructive, and not always unattended with danger,—sufficient, at least, to make it more exciting. So that what would seem to most people to be the entering on a great and perilous voyage in going to South America, becomes, in one of the magnificent hotel-like steamers of the Royal Mail Company, in experience, so pleasing and fascinating, from all the details you meet with, that you terminate your voyage with regret. And when you land and see the strange scenes in the coast cities, and, above all, the splendid and matchless beauties of Rio Janeiro, its harbour, and neighbourhood, you feel it difficult to quit these places; and you also leave with regret the more free, wild, and adventurous scenes of the American "camp."

I strongly recommend a visit of inspection in going

out, if opportunity offers, to Teneriffe, Madeira, Pernambuco, and Bahia. It is worth while visiting the San Francisco River, midway between Pernambuco and Bahia, which is reached from the latter city by a small steamer, that carries you forty leagues up the river to Porto Daspiranhas, where the scenery is grand. You first come to the Salto da Onca, a broken cataract, 600 feet high with its falls. Then, taking mules for 120 miles further, you come to the Paulo Alfonzo, reported to be the finest cataract in the world, where, from the river contracting from a width of two miles, a vast body of water leaps 250 feet down in one fall. Those who have seen it pronounce it superior to the falls of the Nyamsi or to Niagara, which is only 185 feet fall.

From Bahia you have 733 miles voyage to Rio, where a visit of three or four weeks will amply repay you with its unsurpassed and endless natural beauties. You may then look in at the harbour of Paranagua, 200 miles south of Rio, with its wild forest and mountain scenery. Then the Alpine scenery of the neighbourhood of Sanctos will reward your trouble. You next proceed to Monte Video and Buenos Ayres,—large cities, but neither of them much worth seeing, except as specimens of South American Spanish Republican cities, entirely built in squares of houses. You then take to "the camp."

The entire south of the River Plate being a dead interminable flat, with no scenery or rivers, I recommend the north side of the river, which, being hilly and undulating, and intersected with numerous large and small rivers that drain the country for some hundred leagues, is far more interesting. And if you advance much farther north, across the Rio Negro, towards Paraguay, the country is grander and more wild, and most abundant in the large and small game and wild animals.

The return voyage home takes a longer time than in going out, from the trade wind being in this case against you. For the distance of 5700 miles from Buenos Ayres the wind was dead against us, which was an equivalent to 100 miles a day. On going to the seaside in England, you get sunburnt and browned; but after being burnt half black in South America, the sea, on the contrary, restores your complexion to its former state.

I must now conclude the narrative of my travels during nearly a twelvemonth, by expressing the pleasure I have received, and the recollection I shall ever retain of the kindness and hospitality I everywhere met with from the English residents and sheep-farmers, with the hope that, should they return to England, I may meet them and renew my acquaintance with them.

The respective distances from England to the River Plate are as follows:—

Southampton to Lisbon	900
Lisbon to St. Vincent (the coaling station)	1554
St. Vincent to Pernambuco	1620
Pernambuco to Bahia	380
Bahia to Rio Janeiro	733
Rio to Paranagua	200
Paranagua to Monte Video	873
Monte Video to Buenos Ayres	120
Miles	6260

SOUTH AMERICAN

SHEEP-FARMING

AND

EMIGRATION.

IS EMIGRATION DESIRABLE?

WILL IT ANSWER?
AND
WHERE SHALL WE GO TO?

1871.

PREFACE.

THE foregoing queries are points to be ascertained and decided upon by those wishing to emigrate. The United States, Canada, Australia, New Zealand, and Natal have all their zealous advocates and busy agents. But times are altered with these favourite and well-known fields of enterprise.

Any one contemplating leaving his native land will probably have read accounts of settlers that have gone out to "the bush" in Australia or New Zealand, or to "the belt" at the Cape and Natal, or to the woods of Canada. He will have learnt what those settlers did when they arrived there, and he will think he will have to do the same; how a hard-working husband and a thrifty wife bought or rented some wild land; how they raised a little shanty to protect themselves from the rigours of, perhaps, a Canadian climate; and he will have admired the incessant toil and patient endurance they went through, by which they at length achieved for themselves an independence. If his health is not strong, and he is not gifted with the powers of a back-woodsman, the intending emigrant will naturally ask himself—"With this disadvantage how shall I be able to encounter the work of felling trees and clearing the ground of scrub, in order to obtain a piece of virgin land for corn or for a garden?"

I wish, therefore, to draw the attention of those purposing to emigrate, to a country which I regard as immeasurably superior to any of those places to which I have referred. For a man who is young and accustomed to agricultural labour, the place that he may emigrate to is of far less consequence than to one who is not strong, and who is encumbered with a family. The question for him to solve is, can he emigrate to any place abroad where summer is almost perpetual, and but little clothing required; where labour is in high request, and food plentiful (and that found him, with a house to live in); where his work also will be of the lightest kind; and where he can look forward at no distant period to placing himself and those dependent on him in plenty and comfort? Can he hope to realise the happiness of looking on a little estate as his own, with a house raised upon it by his own hands.

This may be, and has certainly been, a true vision of

what many have experienced in our own colonies in past times. Now such a field for emigration is positively to be found and reached at no insurmountable expense or difficulty, as might be imagined, and by the safest and most pleasant of all voyages. The emigrant may go to a country where no toil, such as felling timber and clearing a wilderness of underwood, is necessary,— the land of which is all a rich unenclosed pasture, on the finest soil for pasturing flocks and herds; a sunny land, where the evils of cold climates are unknown; a country that Providence has enriched with every natural advantage, to make it, doubtless, issue hereafter in the grandest development of national prosperity.

Let those interested in the subject, after perusing "The Comparative Sketch of Emigration Fields," read the following statement of what is true at the present time with regard to South America. They will find the conclusion they arrive at instructive, where occupation and health are an object.

DIFFERENT FIELDS OF EMIGRATION COMPARED.

		CANADA.	AUSTRALIA.	SOUTH AMERICA.
1	Price of Passage	£8	£14. 10s.	£8. 10s.
2	Length of Voyage	One Month	Three and a Quarter Months	Two Months.
3	Payment for Labour	Fifty per Cent. higher than England, but in Greenbacks amount to no more	Overstocked with Labourers	£38 Nett.
4	Food	As dear as in England	Fifty per Cent. Cheaper	All Food Found.
5	Labour, Sort of	Fit only for Strong Men	Ditto	Weak Men.
6	Fertility of Land	Good, but Forest	Three Acres to One Sheep	Three Sheep to One Acre.
7	Description	Forest, to be Hewn Down, but Good	Generally Scrub, to be Cleaned	No Labour to Clear Land, all being Fine Pasture.
8	What chance of Emigrants repaying the cost of their Passage	None ever Repay	Ditto	More Probability from Greater Wages.*
9	Lodgings and Food	Food sometimes	Food sometimes	Both Found Free.
10	Health Required	Good and Strong	Good	Labour, being slight, suitable to Weak Health.
11	Price of Land	For Good Land, not under £1-2 per Acre	£1	Six to Eight Shillings for the Finest Pasture.
12	Persons Acceptable	Only Strong and Healthy	Ditto	Any.—Old and Young, Women and Children, all provided for.

* If Government advanced a Loan at Interest, on Parochial Rates (as they can under the Act), to be repaid by Parishes,—while experience proves that nothing is ever repaid by Emigrants sent to Canada and Australia,—far greater probability of repayment exists, when ability to repay from high nett wages is taken into consideration, in those sent to South America.

SOUTH AMERICAN

SHEEP-FARMING AND EMIGRATION.

———•———

In so important a matter as that of leaving England and settling abroad, whether it be from a delicate state of health or to provide a competence, it is very necessary to fix upon a country that presents as many natural advantages and as few objections as possible. Climate, the occupation to be followed, the price of land, the remuneration that may be expected, the cost and readiness of access to it, and the foreknowledge of what disagreeables may be expected, are points that should be carefully weighed.

As I here intend only to allude to South America, I enter no farther on the prospects afforded by other lands, than the brief comparative outline that I give of each; and, therefore, the following pages are to direct those who are totally unacquainted with that part of the world that I here refer to. The sketches that I give of the voyage in another part, and details of incidents of a life in "the camp," will serve to prepare an intending

G

settler for what he may expect to meet with, and the habits and customs he must conform to, when he resides there.

A wrong impression has often been conveyed of South America by either imperfect or by too coloured descriptions, that magnify the advantages to be obtained by going there, or that lessen the evils that exist. That country, with its thousands of square leagues of rich and unoccupied land, has doubtless a great future in store; for it possesses every element and accessory combined for progress and for prosperity to industrious occupants, in a degree far superior to any of our English colonies, and with fewer drawbacks. It has safety of access, and there is food in abundance for any number of emigrants, whilst the climate is as fine as any on earth. At the time I write this I firmly believe no emigration field is available, as many used to be, nor desirable, except South America. The old beaten tracks are overstocked with labour, and some with merchandize; but the continent of which I speak is more in want of hands, and of people of every sort, than of anything else. Here, then, is the cheap market to buy in, as well as the dear one to sell labour in.

The vast tracts of land that lie in the latitude and neighbourhood of the River Plate are watered by the great rivers that run through it—the Uruguay, the Parana, and the Paraguay, and all their tributary streams. Nature is most lavish in the abundance of her choicest gifts in these countries, all of which are now lying dormant for want of inhabitants, and which possess in themselves every natural requisite to support millions of inhabitants in abundance and comfort. Spanish is spoken in the southern and western side of it, and Portuguese in the great kingdom of Brazil, on the eastern.

The Republics of the different Governments, although their institutions are not identical with our own, are yet generally favourable to political and social liberty. A president is at the head of these national governments, who, in conjunction with his cabinet, exercises powers like those of the Great North American Republic. Public opinion is represented by the upper and lower chambers, which possess constitutional control over the proceedings of the executive, for the well-being of all. The utmost freedom and religious toleration exist in these Republics; and in the capitals and chief towns there are English and Scotch Protestant Churches. Broad and enlightened views are held by these chambers, favouring every scheme that tends to the welfare of the people; and they are ready to sanction and promote undertakings that may be brought forward which are conducive to the development of the resources of each Republic.

Among these undertakings may be mentioned the Northern, Western, Great Southern, and Central Argentine Railways. These lines have opened up large and fertile parts of the country, that before had no means of conveying produce to the great seaboard cities—the outlets of commerce—save only by the slow lumbering and unsafe bullock carts.

New tidal docks are opened at the Port of Rosario, which city has 60,000 inhabitants, and will be the future seat of the Buenos Ayres Government. The line of the

Central Argentine is open to Cordova; thousands of acres adjoining it (and there are more still to be bought of the Company at £1 per acre) are brought under cultivation by settlers, and the arrivals are rapidly increasing. And what recommends it especially to English agriculturalists is the increasing facilities for plough cultivation for corn and potatoe crops, hitherto practiced but exceptionally and in very small quantities in other parts, and that by spade labour chiefly.

The telegraph line to connect with the Pacific is in progress, and has been opened to Rio Cuarto, more than half way to Chili.

The Western Railway is a Government line, but the other lines here named have been made by English companies. The most important of these, from its being the longest and penetrating the farthest into the interior, is the Central Argentine, now open for traffic for half its length. It commences at the City of Rosario, situated on the Parana (which is second only to Buenos Ayres in commercial eminence), and will eventually terminate at or near the City of Cordova, the great centre of commerce for the provinces of Rioja, Catamarca, Santiago, Incuman, Salta, Jupuy, as well as Bolivia and Peru. This line will most probably be eventually carried across the Cordillera of the Andes, and will thereby effect a junction with all the cities and states of the west coast of America up to Panama, by the railway system of Chili.

I would here call attention to the fact that the lands of New Zealand and Australia, though deservedly considered as very profitable for raising sheep, are not to be compared with the land of the Argentine Republic, Buenos Ayres, and Banda Oriental. In many districts of New Zealand we have good authority for saying that three acres are required to support a single sheep, and that the fertile lands of New South Wales are capable of supporting one and a-third sheep per acre. In Victoria, where are the best lands, they can support two sheep on every acre. Now if we take this, the most favourable instance, and contrast it with the produce of the regions about the Plate, we cannot fail to be impressed with its peculiar fitness for this branch of pastural industry. Average lands, even on this part of the American continent, will easily support three sheep on an acre; while on that of Buenos Ayres, where the soil is better, four sheep can be maintained in good condition in mid-winter when food is scarcer, and as many as eight in summer before the time of droughts sets in.

But this comparison is still more striking when it is remembered that the lands of Australia and New Zealand have, as a rule, to be cleared of timber and scrub, which is often a labour of toilsome years, before they are fit for grazing purposes; while those of South America are already prepared by the munificent hand of nature for the pasturing of immense flocks and herds.

Another advantage which the Plate has over the Australian continent is its comparative vicinity to the chief centres of consumption for produce, being only half the distance to Europe; and as the means of internal communication are improving, this element of superiority will soon be even more manifest than at present. For raising both cattle and sheep no country can be more productive; and it is capable of indefinite extension. We may also say that the great bulk of the population is engaged in occupations, connected, in one way or another, with this pursuit.

I now proceed to notice, in the order in which they will be most intelligible, the different matters connected with sheep-farming and cattle, which constitute the almost sole occupation of settlers here, and the operations and profits that may be expected.

I. The Measurement and Value of Land.
II. The Climate and Habits of Living.
III. The Time and Plan for Commencing Business.
IV. The Farming Operations and Management.
V. The Prospects.
VI. Labour.
VII. The Sort of Men to Go There.
VIII. Considerations Before Going Out.
IX. Emigration Considered as a Relief from Pauperism at Home.
X. Fields of Emigration.
XI. The Way to Get There.

I. THE MEASURE AND VALUE OF LAND.

The measurement of land in this country, where the Spanish language is spoken, is reckoned by the lagua or by the suerte.

The lagua consists of sixty quadras, by sixty. (Lagua being a league, and quadra a square.) This, when multiplied together to show the extent in superficial measurement of the lagua, gives 3600 square quadras. The quadra is 100 Spanish yards in length. But to bring this into English measurement, that we may know exactly the contents of the Spanish lagua in English square miles, as the Spanish yard is two inches less in length than our yard, the length of one side of a lagua will be 5667 English yards, or 6000 Spanish yards, in length. In other words, a Spanish lagua amounts, in English measurement superficially, to a square of land, each side of which is three miles and about a quarter English in length. The square contents of this will be, say, ten and three-quarters English square miles.

The suerte consists of 2700 square quadras of 100 yards each, which is 4720 English yards long on each side; giving, when reduced in the same way into English measurement, a square of rather more than two and three-quarters English miles on each side, or about seven and three-quarters English square miles.

A square Spanish lagua is therefore ten and three-quarters English square miles, while the suerte is seven and three-quarters.

The estates are bounded on two or three sides, and often on all four sides, by mere mathematical lines, that extend or may be drawn from each of the corners. Rivers or streams are therefore a great advantage as boundaries, to prevent flocks straying. Purchasers, however, are often desirous of having their estanzia or estate re-surveyed, and

then they usually place land-marks at distances of perhaps
a mile, consisting of iron or stone pillars, or of thick upright posts of hard iron wood, called underwaye.   One
estanzia, held by a Scotch Company, has thirty-six land-
marks on a surface of eight square leagues or about eighty-
six English square miles, though many are contented with
mere natural limits, such as a rock or a stream.

The price to purchasers of this land about twenty or
thirty years ago, when it belonged to natives, was almost
nominal.   A fine camp, I know, of three square leagues,
equal to thirty-two English square miles, and bounded
on three sides by rivers, which is a great advantage, was
sold at the end of the last century for 200 Spanish dollars,
or £40.   Not long ago, £18,400 was given for it, with
the stock upon it, by an English firm.   Farther up the
country, an estate of nine square leagues was sold at a
rather earlier date than when the above was, when wild
Indians were upon it, for 250 dollars, or £50.   This would
now be worth 90,000 dollars, or £18,000 English.   So
that, from the time of the last century, the price has
wonderfully increased.   About twelve years ago, a square
league could be bought for 2–3000 dollars, or £500-600,
as the fair and usual price.   But now, and for the last few
years, the regular price for a league has been 14,000
dollars, or £2800; and, for a suerte, 12,000 dollars or
£2400.   And yet, at this greatly advanced price, it only
amounts to seven or eight shillings per acre English (and
cheap indeed, when the rich quality and depth of the soil
is considered); while land is not be had in Australia and
our colonies of good quality for less than £1 per acre, and

which even then is inferior to American. There is also no bush or scrub to be got rid of here, at considerable labour and expense, nor trees, which only grow here at the sides of the rivers, and are useful for firewood. The land here is deep, strong, and fertile.

The rent of land is in proportion to the price. Money on mortgages will produce twelve per cent.; seven per cent. is allowed on deposits in the bank; and land is supposed to produce in rent eight per cent. The usual and fair rent at present of a suerte is 800 dollars, or £160 per annum; although it may be had at 500 or 600 dollars, which is £100–120.

Thus then there is a vast difference between any of our British Colonies and this land, especially when it is taken into consideration that the land in all parts contiguous to the River Plate for a wide extent is as good as can be found anywhere.

II. The Climate and Habits of Living.

The climate of Buenos Ayres, Banda Oriental, Entre Rios, and other parts in the same latitude, is as fine as in any part of the world. Lying, as it does, in from thirty-one to thirty-six degrees of south latitude, a considerable amount of heat may be expected from November to February, that being the hot season of the year, during which the glass ranges from seventy-five to ninety degrees. The mean summer temperature is about seventy-five, and the mean winter about fifty-four; the average annual being about sixty-five degrees.

What makes the climate so healthy is its freedom from any of the sharpness that the air has in England. The air is always soft and mild, and remains almost the same during night-time, when it is not cold as in England, but only a few degrees cooler than during the day. The weather is, in fact, a perpetual sunshine, with nice breezes,—"Buenos Ayres" (good airs), with no changeable weather, and with no extremes from sudden heat to cold, which renders the climate so trying in England.

What has been said of the hottest equatorial and centrical parts of South America may, *in its measure,* be said of countries in the latitude I am speaking of. During a great portion of the year it may be said that "the warmth is not heat, and the coolness is not cold." In the hotter regions, where the glass is never lower than seventy-two degrees, or higher than ninety-five, it has been remarked that these limits include, in each day, spring, summer, and autumn. These are respectively the extreme limits of temperature. So that there is far less variation here than in other climates, and less trial for the constitution.

It is this evenly balanced temperature that keeps the earth's surface ever clothed with unfading beauty and fertility ; and, however superior civilized nations may become in their social relations, by battling with the inclemencies of colder latitudes, yet, from the above-mentioned state of things, we may justly surmise that the most perfect condition of a future race will be attained. *under* or *nearest* to the equator alone; as it is adapted to the most perfect paradise for man's existence upon earth.

As but little difference exists between dry and wet seasons, the days are more like each other throughout the year. The result of this is, that the periodical phenomena of plants and animals do not take place as they do in temperate zones. One who has resided there long, writes, " there is no hybernation here, nor, as the dry season is not excessive, is there any summering season, as in some tropical countries. Plants do not flower and then shed their leaves, nor do birds moult, pair, or breed simultaneously. In Europe, a woodland scene has its spring, its summer, its autumnal, and winter aspects. In equatorial regions, the aspect is almost the same every day of the year. Budding, flowering, fruiting, and shedding leaves are always going on in some species or other. The activity of birds and insects proceeds without interruption. The colonies of wasps, for instance, do not die off annually, leaving only the queens, as in cold climates; but the succession of generations and colonies goes on incessantly. It is never exclusively either spring, summer, or autumn, but each day is a combination of the three. With the day and night of nearly always equal length, the atmospheric disturbances of each day neutralizing themselves before each succeeding morn, with the sun in its course proceeding midway across the sky, and the daily temperature the same within a few degrees throughout the year—how grand in its perfect equilibrium and simplicity is the march of nature under the equator."

In the region of the Plate River (the silver river, not Playte,) there is no such thing as rainy weather of continually dropping moisture, as we have in England. When it

rains, it is a clearing thunderstorm, purifying the air of
abundant electricity, and these in winter are long and
severe storms. One sudden storm that comes on is the
"Pampero," from the vast plains of the Pampas in the
south west. A "temporal," or tempest, may come from
any quarter. Rain begins in April and May in occasional
storms; increasing in June. The cold months are July and
August. At this time, you require some caution in
exposing yourself, as every one is in the habit of wearing but little clothing at other times. In these two
months grass does not grow much, and all stock is leaner
and weaker. In September the weather becomes changeable, and begins to be warm in October, and hot at the end
of it, and still more so in the beginning of November,
when sheep-shearing begins.

As regards the climate affecting people in weak health,
no region can be better suited, especially for throat and
pulmonary weakness. I do not say where positive disease
has made a serious advance, in which case wasting from
the heat might be injurious. I have met, in steam vessels,
medical men who were very consumptive, and who could
only live in such a climate; and, in many cases, where
incipient disease has commenced, a stay of six months
or a twelvemonth has, I know, been strongly recommended, and has effected a perfect restoration to health, all
unpleasant symptoms having disappeared.

The only exception to a continual open-air life is
during the very heavy rains and cold wind (which, being
a *soft* cold wind, is very penetrating) in the depth of the
winter. You then feel inclined to shut close the door and

windows. But even this lasts but very few days, and then not in the middle of the day.

In a perpetual sunshine, with mild air and nice breezes, you enjoy life as you have no conception of in England. The action of such a climate has a corresponding effect on plants and crops. The closeness of the soil retaining the heavy rains causes plants to grow at an incredible rate under the hot-sun. Radishes in a few days will become a foot and a half long, and so thick and wiry that they are uneatable. And hence two crops a year of corn, maize, and potatoes, and six to ten cuttings of alfalfa, which is lucerne, are a common and not unusual thing.

As men in the two hottest months sleep in the middle of the day, the style of living must correspond. You get up at "sunrise." If you have a journey to make, you "gallop" until nine o'clock; and, if the journey is unfinished, you seek shelter from the heat, as well as take refreshment, at some estanzia, or at a rancho (which is a native shepherd's hut), or at a poesta (which is an Englishman's cot), that you happen to meet with, for the middle of the day. Or, if none lies in your way, you unsaddle, throw the reins over the horse's head on to the ground, when he will never move; or you rest under a tree, or in a wood, by the side of a river; and then you complete your journey after six in the evening.

Every one crossing the country in their travels expects accommodation at your house for the night. If you have no catrays, which are X bedsteads, to give travellers, they spread their saddle gear on the floor, and sleep on it as comfortably as they can. Should there be native ladies in the party, you must give up your bed to them. You expect the same at their house, as there are no such things as inns nor shelter of any sort in this open grass country.

You take "matey," which is native tea, or Chinese tea when it is to be had, at "sunrise," with sugar, and with or without hard biscuits and milk. At ten o'clock, you have a substantial breakfast of soup, meat, and wine; and the same at six o'clock in the evening; and, immediately after each, tea is brought in; and you go to bed about half-past nine or ten. Breakfast and dinner are thus the only real meals in the day.

III. THE TIME AND PLAN FOR COMMENCING BUSINESS.

The time you commence business operations depending, as it will do, on the time of the year that you leave England and reach here, will not much signify, if it be only as regards sheep farming.

As sheep shearing takes place in the beginning of November, you will buy stock cheaper after shearing than before it, the difference in price being whether with or without the skin and wool. But, if you wish to have an acre or half an acre broken up from grass into arable land, to grow potatoes or garden crops, or lucerne, in this case it can only be effected at a certain time. And, if you arrive in this country just after that time, you will find that, as regards this piece of ground, a season is lost. And for this reason. There is a very great difficulty in getting land broken up in this country at all. There are no horses answering to our plough horses, of a heavy and slow build;

but all the horses are light riding horses. It is with great difficulty that you get these broken to harness, and especially to the plough. And another difficulty, and a very serious one, is, that even when broken to harness, from the heaviness and closeness of the soil, they can do but little work in a day, from being such light horses. You cannot dig the ground yourself, for the climate will not allow of it, and even natives will find such work too arduous. And, if you attempt to plough the ground when it is too wet, the soil is of such a tenacious nature, that it clings to everything. If you attempt to plough it when it has been exposed to the sun for any time in hot weather, it is then too late; for it is baked as hard as a rock. Therefore, the only time to do this is when the ground is mellow, neither too wet nor too dry. And such a time can only be found in September and April. In some places natives have horses that have been broken and will plough for you, but you must pay dearly for it. It is, however, very indispensable for your comfort that you should have some ground ploughed up; for, if you have none broken up, you may have to go without bread, and you certainly will have to do without potatoes and vegetables.

In the beginning of October your crops must be in. They will grow with great rapidity; and they must be harvested by the end of November or the beginning of December; for the bechamoras, or Spanish fly, makes its appearance then, and it will eat up everything green in your keenta, or garden. In five or six weeks this nuisance dies; and you put in another crop, and harvest it by the end of February.

Therefore, it may be desirable to leave England as winter comes on, when you will escape cold weather, and will arrive out here in summer. You will then see everything under favourable circumstances, and be able to move about and to do many things with greater facility than in winter time, as to distances. You will also have time to look about you, and decide where you will settle.

You should bring some seeds with you, especially garden seeds, as they are very dear here; some tools, such as a spade, hoes without handles, and carpenter's tools, which are very bad and dear here, being generally brought from North America, from whence also are procured ploughs and harrows (which may do), clothes, and goods, which are much dearer here than in England.

IV. FARMING OPERATIONS AND MANAGEMENT.

I shall here speak of this important undertaking strictly as it now exists, under the influence of depressing times, and as carried on by English firms and by single Englishmen; and I will afterwards state the more advantageous way in which the native gentlemen farm, which is more systematic, and therefore more profitable.

To understand what these operations are, it must be borne in mind that this a purely pastural country,—all grass and unenclosed hill, valley, and dale,—with no trees except at the banks of rivers. The pastural occupation is either keeping sheep or cattle. As to sheep-farming, when men first commence, whether they are gentlemen by position or in the grade of the English labourer, they generally go and stay at some English estanzia; and they are kept there for a few months free, where they can learn the duty of "minding sheep," which is soon acquired.

The estanzia farm itself, which we may call the squire's estate, is occupied either by the proprietor himself of this large tract of ground of one or more square leagues, or he is the renter of it, and, as such, he lives in the estanzia house. He lets out the surrounding parts of his land to different shepherds, who are his tenants, each of such pieces having a poesta, or two-roomed shepherd's cottage, upon it. An estate of three leagues will, for instance, have thirty or more poesta lots in it. These poestas, with their portion of land, will generally be let to men who will buy a flock of sheep of the Estanziero, which in these times he is very glad to sell to them. He himself retains the land immediately around the estanzia house for two or three of his own flocks. A flock will number from 800 — 1200, or even more, of ewes of different ages, and a few wethers, called capones.

A gentleman or a labourer, when he has graduated in the business by attending to a flock for a time, buys sheep of the Estanziero according to the amount of his capital, and he settles down in his poesta with a piece of camp, say about a mile square, which he rents for about £20 per annum. But in case he has not capital enough to pay for a flock, besides the rent that he has to pay, he will take another young Englishman as a partner; or he may, either by himself or in conjunction with his partner, take a flock of the Estanziero to mind on half profits, or on thirds, and pay no rent at all. This means that he is to have half or a third of the increase of the flock and of the wool, the Estanziero taking the other portion. In this case he is called a "medianero."

Sheep are also often taken on thirds by the tenant; and many an emigrant without a shilling of capital, and even after having been but a few months in the country, will find no difficulty in finding persons ready to let out sheep on thirds. In this case the medianero, or sheep proprietor, finds the land, the poesta, and the flock of sheep of 1000—1500, of different ages. The tenant gives his personal attention to this flock, and receives every year one third of the proceeds of the increase of the wool and of the skins; and he is allowed to kill, for his own consumption, two sheep a week; and at the end of the third year he receives one third of the increase. In this case he receives no wages, which he would, besides being maintained, if he were only the peon or shepherd of the owner of the flocks. Suppose, then, in three years the original flock of 1500 sheep to have increased to 3000, the increase being 1500, his share will be 500 sheep; besides having been maintained free during the period of that three years.

I know a man who commenced many years ago with 2000 sheep. He married and has a large family grown up. He is now worth 45,000 sheep, besides an abundance of horses and cattle. He farms, on half profits, a large farm of forty-five square miles; and has now sons, able to do the same, who have become managers of large farms.

It is very desirable for young men commencing the sheep business to unite in one firm. Their capital when united will do much more for them than when divided. They are a protection to each other, as well as society; the same house and table serves for all; and they can create a subdivision of labour among themselves, which will save a great amount of fatigue, trouble, and expense.

In the case of being a medianero on thirds profits at the expiration of three years, it is to the advantage of the Estanziero, besides meeting the necessity of the tenant; because as the poestero, or tenant, is interested in the increase of the flock, the Estanziero well knows that for his own interest he will carefully look after the flock. In some cases the Estanziero does not let parts of his camp, from not being able to meet with men who are able to purchase sheep of him. In this case he puts his own peon, or servant, into a poesta, who minds the flock for him, and to whom he pays monthly wages, and keeps him in mutton, yerba, &c., &c. In such case all the profit of the flock belongs to the Estanziero, who for such an office generally selects a native before an Englishman, because he is trained to the business from childhood, and he minds the sheep better. And the man lives and is supported, with his wife and family, by the Estanziero in his poesta.

The duties devolving on this shepherd (who is called a poestero)—or, in fact, of any one minding sheep—are to ride up the sheep *slowly* every evening on to the rodao, or coral, which is a square piece of ground enclosed with fencing in front of the shepherd's cot, where they sleep all night. Plenty of horses are found him for this purpose.

If the sheep are not enclosed in the coral at night, he is obliged to sleep with his little window shutter open, to hear in the night whether the sheep are straying. In this case they might mix with an adjoining flock, which would be a serious case of neglect. Should this happen, he gets up and mounts a horse, one of which is always saddled and ready tethered outside his house, and he rides them up in the dark as well as he can. He must always ride them up slowly; for it takes much out of sheep, as well as out of the horse, to go fast, and is quite unnecessary; especially if the sheep have lambs, which they are apt to lose if hurried.

A young peon will use up horses at a wonderful rate if not prevented from riding them fast, as all young people will do unless prevented. I knew a man who had a small flock, who was obliged to be away for three months. When he came back at the expiration of that time, he found that his three riding horses had been entirely worn out, owing to his young peon having perpetually ridden them too hard.

In the morning the sheep are let out of the coral (if in winter, when the dew is off the grass); and the poestero has nothing else to do during the day but see that they do not stray and mix with other flocks. A man must not have bad sight to do this; and from the wide extent to which sheep spread, many have a binocular glass to see them better at a distance. If two men are in partnership, the duties are divided, which is much better; and also, from the excessive loneliness of the camp, the life they lead is less wearisome. If the poestero suffers his flock, from omitting to watch them, to mix with another, this causes great trouble, and he is deservedly scolded. The consequence then is, that both the mixed flocks have to be driven up to the estanzia coral, and notice being given to both flock-masters, they meet there and go through the process of separating each man's sheep in the presence of the other. This they are able to do by the marks on the sheep, such as slitting the ear, or boring it, or cutting the gristle of the nose. A "mix" more frequently takes place in cold and windy weather, and when the grass is short, than in warm weather; for when the grass is plentiful, in spring and summer, the sheep do not stray at all, and the poestero has literally nothing to do.

During heavy rain and blowing storms, in winter, both cattle and sheep will walk with the storm for leagues, until they are brought up by a river. In these cold storms many perish from the excessive wind and cold; and you may see half a dozen lying dead together, with their lambs. And after a severe night, there will be in the morning a hundred or more lambs lying dead.

If some protection from the severity of the weather were afforded them on these occasions, such as boarding, to shelter them in the coral, numbers might be saved. But as boards are expensive to purchase, and still more so to bring all the way from a town, and the sheep of little value, to endure their loss is the least evil of the two. I must add there exists much carelessness and neglect on the part of the owner.

The sheep will lamb twice a year, and have generally

in times past been allowed to do so. An increase of from
35—50 per cent. may always be fairly reckoned upon;
though I have known, in favourable seasons, good flocks
and camps, 100 per cent. increase in a year. But now
most people prefer not to let sheep lamb more than once
in a year, as it weakens the ewes. The value of a sheep
in November, 1868, and in 1869, was not more, after
shearing (that is without the wool), than half a dollar,
equal to 2s. 1d.

The native sheep are exceedingly inferior as regards
both carcase and wool, the latter not weighing above one
pound. In many cases advantageous results have been
obtained by judiciously crossing indigenous races with
the superior classes of ·Europe; and as formerly the
fleeces of Argentine sheep were meagre and inferior, the
breed has now become heavy and of good quality. The
object in sheep breeding is not merely to breed numbers,
but to get heavy wool, and that of fine quality. The
number bred will depend on the strength and healthiness
of the ewes; and the quantity of wool will depend and
follow on this.

As regards a flock, when you buy them they will
consist of ewes of various ages, and you must not expect to have only two-tooth ewes. It is usual for
the seller to agree for the buyer to draw out fifty from
the flock offered for sale, as objected to for their
inferior character, which have to be replaced by better,
an umpire on each side arranging this. The flock
will consist of so many two-tooth, which are the best
to breed from and the primest, and some that are two

stages older; and, in addition, there will be eighty wethers, or capones, in a flock you buy of 1000. As to rams, you pay so much for putting your ewes to them at the proper season, to the Estanziero, who keeps a separate flock of rams, tended by a peon, by themselves for this purpose. The particular state of the season— a favourable or unfavourable one—has much to do with the prosperity of the breeding flock, and the health and strength of the lambs will depend on the strength of the mothers. In fine seasons, with sufficient wet to keep up the grass, and if the ewes are healthy, you may let them lamb twice a year, and your per centage may be seventy and upwards, without damaging the ewes. I have seen fifty per cent. of fine strong lambs, that were weaned early in February, from one lambing only; but this was the result of the above favourable circumstances being united.

In all this there is nothing parallel to farming on the four-course system of agriculture in England, where the sheep is supposed to produce three crops a year,—in lamb, in wool, and in manure; the last of these being necessary in England for growing roots for supporting sheep, as well as for manuring the ground for seed crops, which are the most paying. But as land here never requires manuring, and is all of it pasture, manure is never thought about.

There is allowed a proportion of fifty rams to a flock of ewes. I once saw 250 rams, with heavy, long, and fine wool in thick folds—the price of each being £60—that were all the offspring of a Rambouillet French ram that had cost £110. The wool of this sort is as fine as silk floss, and five or six inches long. These animals seemed to be suffering greatly from heat, with their heavy coats, which would weigh twelve pounds each. This wool was considered the most valuable sort to breed, from its peculiar fineness and quality, for purposes of making fine cloth. But of late, it being the fashion to wear coarse cloth, it has greatly altered the demand for the fine article. What is now in demand is long coarse wool, more like that of the Cape sheep; and Estanzieros must accommodate themselves to the times by breeding a class of sheep of this description, if they would succeed. It must not, however, be forgotten that a climate like this is not so adapted for heavy-woolled sheep of any sort, as a cold northern climate such as England possesses.

The wool of this country, when exported, contains a heavy per-centage of grease and dirt, which has to be washed out when it comes to Europe. In Australia, they wash the wool, which increases its value. But the scarcity of labourers here renders this too expensive. Lately, an invention has been completed for washing wool, and for carding it by steam; and machinery for that purpose has been sent out to Australia, which will effect a considerable saving in the cost of doing this; but I have heard of none being sent to South America.

With regard to what I have so far stated, and with respect to the present want of prospects, for sheep-farming to become remunerative, which I notice hereafter, under the latter part of this chapter, I must draw a great distinction between the management of sheep under the old-established sheep farmers, natives and semi-natives, and English farmers, especially the Englishmen who have, in later years, come to the country and have engaged in it without the capital, that is sheep and land, and the practical knowledge of natives born and bred to it. Far greater progress and profit will be made by having, not one flock, as most young Englishmen are content to do, but several flocks; and, by working these flocks and disposing of them in the most advantageous manner.

There ought to be *a number of flocks* under one proprietor or firm, at the ratio, say, of ten or twelve poestas and flocks to a square league, which is a square of three and a third miles by the same; and for this purpose, that the younger stock may be placed together, and the older and worn-out, and inferior animals, may be drafted out and killed off every year, to make way for better. So that a continued system of *sorting and drafting* is carried on, to render the flocks of a superior class, and also more land taken in hand and treated, by occupation, in the same way. It must be perfectly clear that a superior average of sheep will be sure to be obtained by a business process of this sort, than by one settler having one flock made up of all sorts, bad, good, and indifferent, and breeding from all alike.

In the few following pages, I am speaking of what is the most effectual and profitable way pursued by the best practical hands, with sufficient land and means. And the only method profitable in difficult times like the present is, that of having the *fullest control* over the whole of the stock. And I here relate the teaching of an able, most experienced, and successful sheep owner.

The breeding ewes must be kept in flocks by themselves, 800 or 1000 in a flock; and weighty-fleeced, heavy-carcased rams should be put to them at the proper season of the year, and that unquestionably is from the middle of October to the middle of December. There must only be one lambing in the year, which will fall, of course, in the autumn. Spring lambs are always an inferior stock; they are checked in their growth by the summer heats, and the loss is enormous in them. Lambs must be drafted out of the flocks and weaned some six or eight weeks before the rams are put to the ewes, which, by that time, will be in the best condition for the purpose.

The ewe lambs must be formed into a flock by themselves—a score or so of old ewes being with them, to keep them together; and when of the proper age (eighteen months), superior rams put to them; the same rams being put to the same ewes every year. This is needful, that uniformity of type, from the several lambings, may be preserved.

The male lambs should be sold off as lambs, or retained in capon flocks, by themselves, until old enough for slaughter,—a given quantity each year being slaughtered.

A portion of the elder and inferior ewe stock should be slaughtered or sold each year, and the number graduated by the increase of the improved ewe stock, for which room has been made.

Following this system, an increase of eighty to ninety per cent. can be, to a certainty, calculated on, from the ewe flocks—half males and half females. Therefore, five flocks of breeding ewes will give each year borregas (that is, lambs of a year old), to form two additional flocks.

The composition of the flocks under this system will be that of animals of uniform age and degree of refinement, and those of the oldest and less-refined ewes will give place each year, in rotation, to a corresponding number of higher bred lambs of one year old. A draft of flocks nearest of age will be made to fill up blanks, from death or disaster, which it may be convenient to make of the least vigorous. Thus there will be no deaths from old age, and few from infirmity of constitution, as the older and weaker will be drafted in course, and slaughtered when they will be at their best. I do not hesitate to say, that twenty per cent. will be saved by this practice alone—a profit of itself—and there will be no degenerate progeny.

In the disposing of the depasturing of the land, the intervening time between the killing off the animals of any given poesta and their replacement by the year-old lambs, taken from the weaning grounds, there will, if a suitable season of the year be chosen, be a growth of grasses which will secure to the young stock a good start, and the seeding of these grasses will keep the camps occupied by the best of them.

Now these things, it is evident, cannot be practised nor their advantages attained where the system of poesteros (that is, flock-masters) *on shares* is adopted. Neither can these things be worked out by small flock-masters, with one or two runs of rented camp. Estanzieros must, therefore, adopt the plan of paying the poesteros a certain sum; and so much per head for the lambs drafted each year out of the flocks under their charge, at weaning time. This will ensure care being taken of the lambs and of the dams, and the best shepherd will gain the most wages.

To work to the best advantage under this system, the land should be fenced, and there should be portions on each run which would serve both for lambing and weaning. In this way, there would be a rest for the grass and a growth of it allowed for the alternately feeding down the land reserved for the best lambs and sheep; and this would give rise to an increased feeding product, which would admit of a much larger number of stock being kept on any given area of land.

Occupying the feeding ground with lambs would be of immense advantage in saving lambs; there would be no driving of the lambing ewes, and no huddling together in dirty corals. The ewes, before lambing commenced, being brought up to the corner of the reserved feeding ground, nearer the house, would, after weaning, come up of themselves quietly, with their lambs; or, at most, would require to be carefully and slowly headed homewards of an afternoon, and would gradually, and according to the strength of the lambs, reach the sleeping ground. There would, therefore, be few desertions and few losses of lambs, and this saving would leave a very handsome return on the capital invested in the fences.

With respect to fences, in all the camps occupied by settlers on the north side of the Plate, excepting one wire cattle fence three miles long across one camp of three square leagues, I never saw any camp fenced, but all left unenclosed, except the keenta, or garden, around

the house and a close of lucerne. Imagine a vast open
country, with no fences or lines of demarcation between
estates of from ten to seventy square miles (except where
rivers bound them), and each of these subdivided to
occupants of single flocks of about a mile square each,
exposed to be continually mixing their flocks from their
straying, and the everlasting riding them back home
again, with, perhaps, a "point," or corner, of a flock
lost by mixing with another, or cut off purposely from
it, and nefariously, by some native, by riding across the
flock for this purpose, besides the waste of labour of
horses and men in such continual riding, and the loss
of ewes in lamb by being driven home too quickly, from
darkness coming suddenly on in the evening, &c., &c.,
and you may imagine the loss from want of fenced-off
pieces of land that so often is sustained, and the consequent want of success and disappointment in farming
that ensues. Yet the excuse with settlers is, "We
cannot afford the expense and labour of fencing." And
most of them, if they could, are too lazy to labour in
making it. This constitutes, therefore, a very serious
item of loss and endless trouble.

It must then strike any reflecting person that the
results of practising farming, as I have before described,
based on principles of care and economical management,
must be widely different from those attainable under the
medianero or share system, or by small flock-masters,
whose flocks are unavoidably composed of ewes of all
ages and all stages of bad condition and constitutional
debility,—year-olds, capones, and lambs dropped at all

seasons,—the whole huddled and scampering together, overrunning, smothering, and losing lambs; the rams running with dam and daughter, sons with dams, brothers with sisters, in every degree of incestuous connexion; the rams themselves debilitated from absence of invigorating food and from excessive and incessant working,—a state of things utterly destructive to breeding, and resulting in constitutional degeneracy and diminution in the yield of wool and carcase products; in fact, resulting in that wretched and discreditable state of things which prevails in the large majority of the flocks of the country, to the ruin of the sheep interests, especially with inexperienced English settlers.

With less than three or four poestas for ewes, and a couple of poestas for lambs and for those of a year old, it is difficult to carry out economically and systematically serious sheep-farming. Probably the smallest scale on which this system which I indicate can be followed out with convenience, and to allow maximum advantages, will be found to be not less than a good half league of land (that is a piece about three and a quarter English miles long by about one and three-quarters wide), with about eight poestas or shepherd's flocks on it. Hence, where land is valuable, small flock-masters must give place to richer.

It is the inevitable course of progress that the smaller men give place to those with the capital and knowledge of the business, sufficient to work on an adequate scale to give maximum results. It is idle, therefore, to work against real estate interests, with the object of bolstering up an undesirable class of men, who do not, and cannot, conduct the sheep industry, which is really a serious consideration to those embarked in it. The scrambling and chance way of letting sheep take care of themselves has now reached its limits, and the sooner men recognize this fact, and prepare to enter on a new plan, the better for themselves and for the interests of the country.

Of course so great a revolution in the practice of farming, as is required to be worked out in a land, cannot be worked out in a day. Still men must struggle on hopefully that it *will* come to pass, though, it is to be feared, not until it is absolutely forced upon them as the only alternative for success.

Let us look at the results attainable under the system I have sketched, and then we shall best be able to judge of the real worth of the land. As to those, both landlords and tenants, who are determined to go on in their old way, nothing more can be said to them than that they are in the certain road to ruin. What we have to say is to those who will listen to, and adopt, a system of improved management. And to such I would lay before them the following assumed sketch of what may be done, what it is possible to do, and what is by no means improbable may be done.

Now, the total estimated number of sheep in the province of Buenos Ayres, in 1865, was 50,000,000, against 18½,000,000 in 1862, showing an enormous increase of nearly *treble* in three years. But the increase, we may assume, has been continuing since in the same ratio; and therefore this fact alone will create competition, and necessitate the more efficient management.

To illustrate the case of good farming, and *brought to nearly present prices* (that is to say, the reduced value of sheep and most remunerative farming, as to per centage of number and weight of carcase and fleece), the following scheme may be considered fair.

Take the basis of a full half league of good land, commonly situated, on which it is proposed to start with a stock of breeding ewes for five poestas of 800—1000 each, say 1000 for round numbers. To gain this end there must be purchased 5000 picked ewes. And to gain these, to the amount of 10,000 or 12,000 mixed sheep must be bought, in order to pick from them the required 5000 in number of ewes and big yearling lambs, called borregas, between the ages of fifteen months and four years. The discarded ones of this 10,000 or 12,000 would have to be run on good camps for a few months, and would, when boiled down for fat, yield back their cost or nearly so. So that the required 5000 ewes would cost, you twenty paper dollars each (a paper dollar is twopence English), or, say, 3s. 6d., to which you would have to add the cost of threepence each for dipping them twice or thrice, so as radically to cure them of the scab—a step of prime necessity—before putting them on the ground, which should have been kept free of stock, and especially of scabby sheep, for six or eight weeks before moving on to it. Of course sheep should be selected before rams were put to them, or otherwise all the lambs, male and female, must be sold for the market; for it must be understood that the object of the sheep farmer should be to breed improved stock.

As there would be a difficulty in getting the whole of the ewes without being in lamb, we will assume that the majority are in lamb purchased at the beginning of the year. Or, take the following calculation:—Suppose that, in January, 1871, they stand on the ground, and perfectly cured of scab, 5000 ewes, costing three shillings and nine-pence each, or £938; if the sheep-farmer knows his own interest, he will put to these ewes, in the coming spring, really good rams, weighty in carcase and fleece. Such rams are not easily obtained in any number, and it is hardly to be supposed he could obtain suitable ones under an average of £12. 10s. each. Eighty of these will cost £1000.

After this, assuming that the majority of the ewes are in lamb, he will have for the market, between June and August, 1871, 2500 lambs, at two shillings and sixpence each, worth £312. 10s., male and female. Of course, he would not keep any that were underbred. In November, 1871, he will shear 5000 ewes, which, if they have been early and well cured of the scab, and, if all are young and picked ewes, their wool would run six fleeces, making one aroba (twenty-five pounds in weight). This, at fivepence half-penny per pound, would amount to £467. The eighty rams' wool averaging ten pounds each ram, at sevenpence per pound, say £23. 10s.—total of three amounts, £803.

In October, 1871, the sheep-farmer will put his own prime rams to his 5000 picked ewes and year-old lambs, from which he may (under the system indicated) fairly calculate on eighty or ninety per cent. of lambs. There can be no question of this result, if the rams are vigorous and well fed, and the ewes in suitable condition, which they will be if the Estanziero knows his business. Therefore, before the end of May, 1872, he will have, at the rate of eighty per cent., 4000 healthy lambs, having made allowance for some losses. Having these 2000 ewe lambs and 2000 tup lambs, an Estanziero, with half a league of land, will find it more convenient to sell his tup lambs than to keep them for capones (wethers), as he can thereby make more flocks of breeding ewes. Therefore, in and before August, 1872, he will have realized 2000 male lambs at, say, two shillings and sixpence each, equal to £250. In November, 1872, there will be shorn 5000 ewes and eighty rams, equal to £467 and £23. 10s. At the end of August there will have been weaned 2000 ewe lambs, which will, in October, be formed into two flocks occupying two additional poestas, which will be shorn or otherwise, as thought best. We will assume they are not shorn as lambs this time. In October, the rams will have been again put to the 5000 ewes.

In August, 1873, there will be, on the same calculation as above, 2000 male lambs at two shillings and sixpence each, equal to £250. In October there will be 2000 weaned ewe lambs for two poestas, one being additional (making eight) and one to replace the poesta of the oldest thousand of the 5000 original ewes, which should be in prime condition in November for slaughter, and they will yield their original cost from their grease and full-woolled skins.

In November, 1873, these 1000 ewes to be realized for slaughter will fetch say, at three shillings and sixpence each, £175. They will be shorn with the 4000 that are kept of the original stock, the 5000 together producing £467, at about three and a-third pounds each sheep. There will also be the wool, as before, of the eighty rams, equal to £23. 10s.

So that, on this principle of getting the best stock to keep, drafting off the oldest and inferior, increasing and adding the prime young ewes, to occupy additional poestas and to constitute more flocks, on the plan of having the most efficient and healthy breeders, all with the object of occupying the whole half league of camp originally but partially occupied, will, if the seasons are good for a few years, result in doubling the stock or capital, besides interest on the outlay and keep of the sheep-farmer.

Now this will be better seen by reducing the subject to figures in outgoing and profit account. We will assume the capital embarked to be £2000, thus :—

At the beginning of the year 1871, after having weeded out and sold 5000 of the most inferior of the 10,000 bought—so as to get at the object of having 5000 prime breeding ewes,—the cost of sheep will be :

	£	s.	d.
5000 prime ewes, at three shillings and ninepence, with threepence each for dipping - - - - -	£937	10	0
80 rams, at twelve shillings and tenpence	1000	0	0
	£1937	10	0

H 2

The first year, 1871—

OUTGOINGS.

Rent of half league	£90	0	0
Five peons, or shepherds, at £37	185	0	0
Shearing 500	31	0	0
Interest, ten per cent. on capital	200	0	0
400 capones, for killing	80	0	0
Sundries	40	0	0
	£626	0	0

PROFITS.

Clip of 5000	£467	0	0
Clip of eighty rams	23	10	0
400 skins, at 1s. 6d.	30	0	0
Increase of 2000 ewes and 2000 young rams, at 1s. 6d. each, not sold	300	0	0
	£820	10	0

Second year, 1872—

OUTGOINGS.

Rent	£90	0	0
Interest of capital	200	0	0
Five peons	185	0	0
Two additional, from August	20	0	0
500 capones, for killing, at 4s. each	100	0	0
Sundries	35	0	0
	£630	0	0

PROFITS.

2000 yearling male lambs, sold at 1*s.* 6*d.*	-	£150	. 0	0
Sixteen months' wool	-	-	-	-	150	0	0
1000 oldest ewes' fat, in November -	-	175	0	0
Wool of 5000	-	-	-	-	-	467	0	0
Wool of eighty rams	-	-	-	-	23	10	0
					£965	10	0

The system will be continued on the increasing plan of these two years, selling off the young male lambs and also the oldest of the ewes first bought, and creating increasing flocks of prime young ewes to occupy the remainder of the half league. And when the whole half league is thus filled up, the capital originally embarked will be fully doubled, after paying all expenses, and providing an ample supply of meat from capones, which I have charged as an item, to simplify it in the outgoings. Farmers in England generally expect a return of fifteen per cent. invested in farming in all its branches put together. I have here charged interest on the £2000 capital at ten per cent.

Now I believe this to be practicable under the favourable conditions of sufficient capital, perfect management, and good seasons, and, by not attempting to farm sheep on the wretched one-flock principle, with very little capital. One serious item is the weather. Either very wet weather will kill sheep, which are always unprotected, by hundreds—especially if they are a weak stock—or, if there comes on a seco or drought, they are starved; which latter casualty seems periodically to happen after a certain number of years.

that market for wool altogether, which was the principal market.

The rich Estanzieros who in times past made hay while the sun shone, may live comfortably enough with their 40,000—70,000 sheep, besides cattle, and having no rent to pay. But I know many cases where English settlers in a smaller way are on the verge of ruin and bankruptcy; and, what is worse, they are without the means of returning home and beginning life once more in England again.

Estanzieros will be glad to sell sheep to any one that will buy them; but they will probably caution young men just come out—as I know in several instances they have done—on no account to embark in sheep-farming, and will tell them that if they do they will never again see their money so invested.

It is perfectly clear that for a man to commence farming sheep at the present selling price would be madness, unless, through some great ruin of the land-owners or land-holders, land was to sink to its real relative worth compared with the present value of sheep. This ought to be at less, or at certainly not more, than its value was nine years ago, which was 2500—3000 dollars as the purchase price for a suerte, or £40 sterling rent.

It may be said, if you can always sell cattle that are fat to the jobbers to sell in town, why not give up sheep-farming and keep cattle only. But cattle will not pay as sheep used to pay; and it is not a pursuit much sought after as an occupation. Ten years ago, when men had

To Expenses of third year:—Same as in
    the second - - - - -   189 12 0

  ,, Expenses of fourth year:—Four poestas,
    four peons, four sheep-pens, and four
    horses, at above rates - - -   252 16 0

  ,, Expenses of fifth year:—Five poestas,
    five peons, five sheep-pens, and five
    horses - - - - - -   316 0 0

  ,, Balance profit from below - - -   9105 12 0

INCOME.

By principal of 5000 ewes—

Increase of	Males.	Ewes.	Total.	Arobas of Wool.	£	s.	d.
First year	1250	1250	2500	500..	200	0	0
Second year ..	1500	1500	3000	750..	300	0	0
Third year ..	2000	2000	4000	1000..	500	0	0
Fourth year ..	2500	2500	5000	1400..	770	0	0
Fifth year	3500	3500	7000	1800..	1080	0	0
			21,500		£2850	0	0

Value of increase, at two and a-half dollars
    (the then value) - - - - 10,750 0 0

                                 13,600 0 0

Say less for eventualities - - - 1600 0 0

      Nett profit, as per contra - - £9,105 12 0

that market for wool altogether, which was the principal market.

The rich Estanzieros who in times past made hay while the sun shone, may live comfortably enough with their 40,000—70,000 sheep, besides cattle, and having no rent to pay. But I know many cases where English settlers in a smaller way are on the verge of ruin and bankruptcy; and, what is worse, they are without the means of returning home and beginning life once more in England again.

Estanzieros will be glad to sell sheep to any one that will buy them; but they will probably caution young men just come out—as I know in several instances they have done—on no account to embark in sheep-farming, and will tell them that if they do they will never again see their money so invested.

It is perfectly clear that for a man to commence farming sheep at the present selling price would be madness, unless, through some great ruin of the land-owners or land-holders, land was to sink to its real relative worth compared with the present value of sheep. This ought to be at less, or at certainly not more, than its value was nine years ago, which was 2500—3000 dollars as the purchase price for a suerte, or £40 sterling rent.

It may be said, if you can always sell cattle that are fat to the jobbers to sell in town, why not give up sheep-farming and keep cattle only. But cattle will not pay as sheep used to pay; and it is not a pursuit much sought after as an occupation. Ten years ago, when men had

To make such a table (and a very unusual one it is)
worth calculating, the amount of increase of 20,000 sheep
in five years, at 4s. each would be - - £4000 0 0
Five years' wool - - - - - 2770 0 0

                                        ————————————
                                        6770 0 0

Less original cost 5000 sheep £1000 0 0
Five years' expenses of peons,
    rent, poestas, and horses - 1982 0 0—2982 0 0

                                        ————————————
                                        £3878 0 0
                                        ————————————

Five years' profit, instead of £9105. 16s.

But here comes one fact that knocks down all this
calculation of profits of £3878, and that is, that you
cannot sell sheep for farming purposes, because there is no
demand for them. The only profit you can expect to get
from them, as a rule, besides their wool and skin, is the
grease you get by boiling them down.

Farming cattle, instead of sheep, does offer remuneration.
The cattle are rather less in size than English cattle,
and are generally sold by the herd of 200—800, at 14s.
per head, including yearlings. The profit from farming
cattle is less than what has been derived from sheep in past
times. It has not varied as the value of sheep has done. It
has usually been reckoned at twelve per cent. on the capital
embarked, while sheep have been averaged at twenty-two per
cent., though this last has greatly oscillated. It is a safer
investment, and one that requires nothing like the trouble

of sheep. Because when the cattle are fat, in the summer, from November to April, there is always a sale for them at £2 a head to dealers who drive them up for the butcher in towns. The skin of a cow is worth a dollar.

Keeping cattle will depend in some measure on the nature of your camp. If the ground lies damp, with long wiry grass, or has broom growing upon it, the cattle will eat all this, while sheep will not. In some places more than in others they are subject to a disease that maddens them, of which they soon die. When in this state, even as young beasts, they will charge anything that goes near them, though they seem to lose the power of moving many yards, and are soon obliged to stop. Some difficulty is found at first in " carenching " or naturalizing them to a new place. Therefore, it is well to buy cattle, if you can, on a camp that you enter upon to rent. Natives are cruel enough to cut the hoofs of the cattle to the quick, to prevent them from straying. The entire country being unenclosed, the wild cattle (which are *supposed* to belong to natives) roam about in thousands everywhere. If you have much stiff long grass on your camp, they will do it good by eating it down; but if not, they must be hunted off your camp continually, until they forsake it, with a couple of " cattle dogs," which you must keep for the purpose.

Let no one, then, now going out, attempt to sink himself in the difficulties that sheep-farmers (I speak here especially of Englishmen) are now involved in, by embarking in sheep-farming. In a district I was in for nearly a twelvemonth, of about eighty miles by seventy, which I constantly rode over, I find that since I left it, nearly half the sheep-farmers have failed, and are sold up and gone away.

If an Englishman must go out, let him take out with him a steam boiling-down apparatus, which costs from £150 —£250, and he will not only do well himself, by boiling down the sheep of the residents, at so much per head, but he will be conferring a great benefit on the farmers, by providing for them an outlet for their produce, because the *fat* of sheep will *always command a sale*. The man who will set up this business *will always obtain* good remuneration. Whilst the sheep-farmer will likewise obtain a profit, though very small, out of his sheep, by having access to means for converting them into a marketable produce (which is impossible at present), for hardly any steam-boiling apparatus exists on the camp anywhere. Estanzieros who have abundant sheep to get rid of, will have constant recourse to such an establishment, and the owner's profit is certain. A single man may follow this pursuit, but he will require several men to help him. But, if three or four were to combine and unite themselves into a firm, the business would be more successful; because one member of the firm might be engaged in moving about, making purchases of flocks to be delivered to the buyers, at the boiling-down place; and, from the difficulties that beset farmers here, sheep are offered constantly at very low prices indeed. This would bring in an additional source of profit. As to the ordinary business of the establishment, Estanzieros would be only too glad to sell them thousands of sheep, and to rid themselves of their surplus stocks at -

the barest profit, by paying so much a-head for boiling them down. The other partners could superintend the work itself of converting sheep into grease, and packing it off for exportation.

In spite of what I have so far stated as to sheep-farming being so generally successful in past times, and especially so under native management, with plenty of good flocks, and land, and that the contrary to all this (leaving the present times out of the question) is one great source of want of success with English settlers, it may be asked what prospects are there to induce persons wishing to settle here in sheep-farming to do so? I must candidly reply there is at present none whatever. There are some who have known the country in past successful times who will deny what I am now going to say.

I will now mention what I believe as to

V. The Prospects.

Men accustomed to olden times form their ideas of the present state of things from what they have experienced themselves in years gone by. They are unwilling to give up these impressions ; and they forget that countries developing by colonization and emigration are continually altering, and that sheep-farming also is liable to be greatly altered from the conditions being changed that used to prevail.

For instance, a man some years ago could make money by selling sheep at good prices. Now he cannot sell at very low prices. Any one going to South America must find, as an actually existing fact, that sheep farmers are on the verge of ruin, with no sale for their stock (every one being overstocked), and with sheep offered at 1s. 8d. to 2s. 1d. each, and no buyers; and, moreover, with land at the *highest renting price* ever known in this country,—two opposites, utterly destructive of success.

Now, the proof of this is remarkably clear and unmistakeable. For instance, some years ago sheep were worth three dollars apiece, or 12s. 6d., while the rent of land was then £40 per annum for a suerte. Now sheep are worth 2s. apiece, and land is rented at £160 the suerte. In other words, sheep were worth *seven* times the value *then* that they are *now ;* with land at *one-fifth* the cost that it is at present.

This is, indeed, a wonderful discrepancy in the relative value of produce and the price of rent; for sheep ought now, at the same ratio of rent for land, to fetch five times the amount that they *formerly* did, as the rent has risen that much. This would amount to £3 apiece, instead of their actual price of 2s. Such an extreme revolution in the value of stock and rent of land takes place in no other line of business in these times; and this will account for the utter depression that now exists. Sheep farmers have now no other resource to look to, to maintain themselves, but their wool money. And what adds to the present depression is, that wool, instead of fetching from 1s. to 1s. 8d. a pound, as it formerly did, does not now realise more than 6½d. a pound for the very best. This arises from the North American Government having laid on a duty of twenty-five per cent. on wool, which has in a great measure shut up

that market for wool altogether, which was the principal market.

The rich Estanzieros who in times past made hay while the sun shone, may live comfortably enough with their 40,000—70,000 sheep, besides cattle, and having no rent to pay. But I know many cases where English settlers in a smaller way are on the verge of ruin and bankruptcy; and, what is worse, they are without the means of returning home and beginning life once more in England again.

Estanzieros will be glad to sell sheep to any one that will buy them; but they will probably caution young men just come out—as I know in several instances they have done—on no account to embark in sheep-farming, and will tell them that if they do they will never again see their money so invested.

It is perfectly clear that for a man to commence farming sheep at the present selling price would be madness, unless, through some great ruin of the land-owners or land-holders, land was to sink to its real relative worth compared with the present value of sheep. This ought to be at less, or at certainly not more, than its value was nine years ago, which was 2500—3000 dollars as the purchase price for a suerte, or £40 sterling rent.

It may be said, if you can always sell cattle that are fat to the jobbers to sell in town, why not give up sheep-farming and keep cattle only. But cattle will not pay as sheep used to pay; and it is not a pursuit much sought after as an occupation. Ten years ago, when men had

their flocks increasing fifty per cent. per annum, and when they could sell their increase (the sheep being worth three dollars, or 12s. 6d., apiece) at that price, the business was like coining money. And with many that have left the country some years, and have come home, the history of this is not forgotten, but is supposed to be still existing; and men will even argue that it is. Any one, however, hazarding the attempt will soon learn to his cost how completely the tables are now turned. And John Bull, when unsuccessful and in distress, and, perhaps, insolvent, with the native bailiff selling him up for rent that he cannot meet, will feel most miserable in a land teeming with plenty, and sigh for old England again.

If any one, then, asks me what prospects there are in the immediate present time or in more distant, I must honestly say that I can see none in either. I do not see how it is possibly to be hereafter even, until a complete revolution in the present state of affairs has taken place, and things shall have once more found their proper level. Then, and then only, may the case be altered. I mean by this, that supply and demand must be properly regulated, like everything else, for a healthy state of this trade to take place. Where there is a too great preponderance on either side, the balance will be uneven; and this must be by some means adjusted. If sheep are still to be produced at the present ratio, some enormous demand must be made for them from some new quarter or other, or the supply must be lessened; and I see no chance of this as things are going on; and that supply, instead of diminishing, is rapidly increasing in the multitudes of sheep that are created.

Therefore, as there are two things at present in fault that make sheep-farming unsuccessful,— high rent of land and low value of sheep,—to make the matter more even, that the settlers may obtain, say, only a moderate profit (supposing they *can* find a market for sheep), land must come down greatly. The Government also of the country, instead of taxing sheep at their former value of fifteen rials, or a dollar and a half, per head, must value them at not more than half of this. Also, if the North American wool duty should be lowered, which is not likely in the face of their great national debt, this may assist in the creation of some marginal profit on the sale of wool.

It is perfectly clear that unless some unforseen change takes place, such as the discovery of means to send meat fresh to England, sheep never can again command the price they have done in time past. Against the sheep farmer there is rent, sheep tax, and peons' wages remaining at the same price (the rent being even far higher) as when sheep would bring two and a half or three dollars a head. If sheep have sunk under a dollar a head, how is a profit to be possibly made, or a certain loss to be avoided?

Look at the position in which men entering on the business are now placed, and must be. When you take a piece of camp to rent, the rule is to stock it with about one-third of what it will sustain, to allow of food and room for the increase of the flock. I know men who began on this plan some years ago, who paid three dollars a head for their sheep. Suppose they have from that time to this trebled their flock, or made them four or five-fold the number, their flock now is positively worth less than when they first bought them. And what is more, their land is as full as it will hold; and they must get rid somehow of the surplus, for every one is in the same dilemma.

Some will say that by boiling down you can get fifteen pounds of fat, worth twopence a pound, from a sheep, besides its skin and its wool; but I have it on the authority of one who has boiled down some thousands of sheep, that it is proved that you cannot average more than twelve pounds of fat per sheep at the *very fattest* time. At other times eight or ten pounds would be the average, and in winter almost nil. Besides this, steam boiling *apparati* do not exist in the camp; and, therefore, they are totally inaccessible to the great majority of the farmers; for a fat flock would waste considerably in being driven to these places from long distances. If, by boiling down, or by any other means, sheep can be made to produce one dollar a head, rents ought still to come down. It is a millstone about these settlers' necks. But so long as Englishmen will create a competition for land, with either native landlords or with large Estanzieros, these prices are not likely to be reduced.

But a man is not obliged to farm sheep in this country. He can direct his attention to many other things, and he can make a comfortable existence by other pursuits. If he has capital, more or less, he will find various openings turning up for speculative business in various ways. If he has only his own labour to look to, without any capital, various trades are in great request. A wheelwright is not to be met with in the camp: and the charges for repairing carriages, gigs, and carts (the two former being brought from North America) are enormously high, and the cost of them when new in proportion. The same remarks will apply to carpenters, who get two and a half to three dollars a day, or 10*s.* 6*d.* to 12*s.* 6*d.*, besides bed and board, as is in all cases usual. Shoemakers are also in great request. A handy man, who can turn his hand to anything, can soon earn handsome wages. If he brings out from England a small moveable forge on wheels, such as they have on board ship, he will find plenty of work at every estanzia, in repairing iron things, *at his own prices.*

I am free to allow that much of what I have described throughout will depend on the different points of view from which they are regarded. Yet there are certain facts and realities that are indisputable, and any deduction arrived at must be based upon these.

VI. The Labour.

As to labour, it must not be thought that there is anything like the regular labour of England. Labour properly so called may be said not to exist here. In Paradise, even, man had to labour and cultivate the ground; and out of Paradise ever since labour has been a hard necessity; but it is not so here. An Englishman carries his home ideas abroad, and thinks he will have to do the same work, in the same manner, and with the same tools as at home; and, in addition, to have better food, and have the same drink. He will soon find he must give up such notions. He need not be one ac-·customed to heavy labour,—to use the axe, mattock, or spade; he may be a town artisan, or even a stove-bred man, unused to arduous toil and shrinking from winter cold. This is the man suited to the light occupations of the country.

After once some posts are fixed upright in the ground, and a roof is fastened on them, with thatch or iron sheets nailed on it, and the walls wattled and daubed with black clayey mud, or else built up with turfs, and when some fencing has been made round it, the emigrant is free from what to many is a terrible duty. For sitting at the door of his humble cot, and seeing that the sheep do not stray, is all he has to do if he is a poestero or shepherd.

A weak man, incapable of hard work, is just as good for occupation like this as the strongest, and can earn as much wages. A man who has no capital, or who is unwilling to mind sheep, can become a cook in a household at the usual " ounce a month." The men that do this are usually not of the most respectable class; though I have seen sons of clergymen and of officers in our army act in this capacity, and sit down at table with you after they have cooked and brought in the dinner.

· Sheep-shearing is an important business. Every peon desires, and is expected, to help at shearing time, which is at the end of October or beginning of November; both because it is difficult to get enough hands to shear so many sheep, and because a man earns more by this than by his usual wages. Every man is paid about five farthings per sheep for shearing. The average number that a man can shear a day is from fifty to seventy.

At this time shearers have additional tea and some cannia allowed, besides the usual meat. There is a division of labour in this work. The Estanziero stands in the middle of the "galpond," a sort of barn adjoining the sheep coral, with a bag of round bits of tin, handing one to each man as he finishes a sheep. Two others roll up the fleeces in a ball, tying them tight, and throw them to another, who stands at the side of a long wool bag that is suspended between two beams, with the bottom of it touching the ground. This last man throws the parcels of wool up into the bag; while another inside the bag keeps trampling the balls of wool down, to pack them tight, until the bag is filled. These bags of wool are sent off to another estanzia, that has a hydraulic press, for compressing them into the smallest compass, binding them also with hoop-iron in square bales from four to five feet cube by six long, weighing seven or eight hundredweight, when they are ready to be sent off by bullock cart to the coast, for shipment to Flanders or North America.

Now, when it is considered that a man who is incapable of hard work in England is here provided with a house to live in, and with food for himself and family, in a beautiful climate; that, if well conducted, he is sure to be treated well; and that he can lay by his wages, amounting to £37 or £38 per annum, at seven per cent. interest in the bank; enabling him, in two years' time, to become proprietor of a flock of sheep himself, and, perhaps, also to take charge of an additional flock of his master's, for which he will get paid; what, I ask, can equal this in any part of the globe at the present time? For, however unprofitable sheep-farming may be to the proprietor, as it certainly is now, still the peon is paid the same wages, and must be, or the sheep would be lost; so that his wages never lessen.

VII. The Sort of Men to Emigrate Here.

A young English gentleman who is unaccustomed to labour and who has weak lungs, if he has a small capital, may pass his time in South America comfortably as regards his health. There many diseases disappear at once. All throat affections and lung disturbances cease. I speak this from positive knowledge. I do not mean to say that a man in an advanced stage of consumption ought to go there, if his complaint is fixed upon him; but where there is a tendency to consumption, and even a strong one, the change becomes at once so beneficial that it is almost incredible. His small capital invested in sheep will maintain him, but no more; for, as sheep are not now convertible into money, he must consider the money sunk in them as lost if he wishes to leave the country.

An idle man, who will not attend to business, had better not go there at all. He will soon find out that no one wants his company, and he will be looked upon as a mere loafer, and will at last have to descend to most menial services, ending, perhaps, in being a drunken castaway.

But the case is very different with a sober and in-dustrious man. If I were asked to point to a quarter of the world that Providence seems to have destined to be the greatest, most successful, and glorious, so far as the country and its natural productions are concerned, it seems to be this. It is here that all that is needful for the welfare of the human race is capable of being produced in the greatest plenty. The climate is the finest, with perpetual summer and no wet weather. Here you may eat food without scarceness, mutton being at a mere nominal price; and you may get double heavy crops of potatoes and maize, and that from ground that requires no manuring.

VIII. Considerations Before Going Out.

Before people leave England with a view of settling abroad, there are many things that ought to be seriously and carefully considered. As a rule, with those that emigrate, most people go abroad with the expectation of thriving well and of making a comparative fortune, and then returning to live in independence after a certain number of years. And I think that, subject to providential and unforeseen occurrences, a man may reasonably expect to do so; and he is not expecting too much in thinking to accomplish this if he sets about it in the right way. Unless he can effect this, and if he is to struggle under difficulties abroad, no matter in what country, he had much better struggle on under such difficulties at home, and save himself the trouble of going abroad.

Two plans seem necessary to be estimated in emigrating, either by State or by other aid, which are, *to go out as a settler*, or *to go out as a working man*, not settling down in one fixed spot.

As our Government will only aid emigration to one of our colonies, if you go in this way, free of expense, it will be as an artizan or a labourer,—say to Canada, where wages are higher than in England. But I cannot see that this will afford you any opportunity for ultimately effecting what I have mentioned above,—a future independence. From what I have learnt from intelligent men whom I have met with from all parts of the world, I have but one conclusion to arrive at, which is, that success will not attend emigration at present in any quarter of the world. It is a failure everywhere. Things are so different to what they were in former times. I yet hesitate not to say that South America is the only exception to this. It is a place where a sober working man (one, be it remembered, who is not strong) may obtain a certain independence in a very short time. I here speak of him not as a renter or fixed settler, but as a mere peon or servant.

If he goes out as a *settler* in a wild and distant spot, one thing is absolutely necessary, and that is, that he should have sufficient to maintain himself and family until he can earn money, or he will be exposed to terrible hardships. The other part of the business will come readily enough, if this is provided for, from some quarter or other.

I knew an instance of a number of emigrants who were landed upon the bare ground that had been provided for them, but for whom no provision was made in the way of food and lodging. This was on a fine part of the coast of South America. The consequence was that they went through great sufferings, barely escaping starvation for the first year, and sleeping for a long time on the ground, *sub Jove aperto*. But, having by great industry and most strenuous exertions surmounted the first preliminary steps, they rapidly succeeded, and they are now a comfortable and thriving colony, with plenty of bread, butter, milk, beer, and meat, and are also well clothed. So that, in the case of emigrants not going out as labourers to other people's houses, but as settlers on new ground, unless the first step is taken of providing a maintenance for the first six or twelve months, none ought to go out as settlers on land. And no one with the common feelings of humanity ought either to persuade others to go, or should take part in promoting their going.

Another thing necessary before leaving England, if you value your life, is to be carefully examined by a medical man,—one especially who has been in hot countries and who knows the complaints to which Englishmen or Europeans are more particularly liable to, from exposure to heat and to the habits of hot climates. You should ascertain if there is any disease existing, especially in the vital organs, such as the liver and the kidneys. These are sure to trouble you and to bring on confirmed disease, and, perhaps, death, if you remain exposed to exciting causes in a foreign land, when you may not have the means of reversing the step you have taken.

It is a common thing for a man at middle age of life to be so affected by the climate that, if neglected, it will be sure, from a continued residence there, to end fatally; while younger persons become easily acclimatised, and feel no ill effects from a change of climate. I refer to a change of residence from a temperate or a cold climate to a tropical one.

Another thing—more useful, perhaps, than necessary—is, that abroad you must endeavour to divest yourself of English prejudices and home feelings. You must not persist in thinking that the customs of foreign lands are necessarily wrong because they do not coincide with what you are accustomed to at home. It must be accepted generally that the habits and ways of doing things in these places are those that are best suited for them. It must be taken for granted that the difference in climate, heat, and weather necessitate customs that seem strange and uncouth to us, but which experience has proved to be both right and necessary. Do not, therefore, too readily condemn everything that seems odd. Many things abroad, it is true, are foolish and barbarous, and may be remedied with advantage; but these must be distinguished from what the climate renders indispensable.

The chief point to be remembered is the change you will have to encounter in food and habits; and that to live in health and comfort you must conform to what the natives of the place do. One chief difficulty you meet with in coming here from a temperate to a tropical zone is how you are to satisfy thirst, which is increased by heat. If you expect to do this with beer (which is an English

habit) you will find it impossible, with very rare exceptions;
for beer is not to be had, because it is not made in hot
countries; nor is it prudent to habituate yourself to
cannia, however diluted, as the taste grows upon you.
But you must quench your thirst with water or tea, and
keep up your strength with plenty of meat, an abundance
of which is everywhere used, and is to be obtained at
merely nominal price.   Chinese tea and yerba, the native
Brazilian tea, is readily obtained.   Labour in this hot
relaxing air can only be endured for a very short time—
I may say minutes—and that only in winter.

IX. Emigration as a Relief for Pauperism at
Home.

X.   Fields of Emigration.

It is acknowledged on all hands at the present period
that it is desirable to find a good field for emigration
for our redundant population.   It is an undoubted fact
that our poor rates are increasing, and that the question
of poor relief is approaching the formidable form and crisis
that it did formerly.   And we must feel assured that if
the present state of things go on, poor rates must be
doubled, simply because pauperism will be in the course
of time.   It should also be borne in mind that the difficulty of remedying the evil, when it has accumulated and
grown, will be increased even in a greater ratio than that
increase.   To prevent such an evil before it grows much
larger is evidently more prudent than when it has expanded
into an enormous extent.

The question is, how is this to be done? Is it to be done by Government aid in promoting emigration, or is it to be done by the efforts of private charity?

Now our Government has laid down a rule from which it will not depart, and that is to afford (or rather I might say, take into consideration the affording) aid to emigration *only to our colonies,* and not to a foreign country. Canada —from its nearness, its being easily reached, and at a lesser cost, its being peopled with English, and from its requiring labourers—presents the readiest field.

But, does Canada present an unexceptional field?. Supposing it will give to English labourers who are sent there fifty per cent. more wages than they get in England, will this be a sufficient inducement for men to go there, in the face of a severe Canada climate, that will kill the weakly ones? Besides, our colonies naturally resist the exportation to them of sickly persons, as they require strength for labour. One class is, therefore, excluded from going there.

The utmost then, that we can say of Canada, is that it will place healthy and strong men, and those only, in the same position that they would be in England, with constant wages at an increase of fifty per cent. And Canada can offer them no more. There must also be some limit to the number, even in this case.

But what is this compared with South America, where any number of men are wanted? Not merely strong men, but any multitude landed on those shores are gladly received, and man, woman and child are readily provided for in work in that vast continent, which can absorb any number.

I have seen thousands of every age land here from the Basque provinces of France and Spain. They are a steady and industrious class of men, and all do well. You see two or three "Basques" standing in the corners of every quadra in the towns, with their hemp slippers on, and a small bag across their shoulders, ready to be hired to carry loads; and these men are all provided for, with their families, either in the towns or in the country.

The opportunities offered for emigration to English colonies are limited, and there is no certainty of a competence to be expected; but, in South America, they are unlimited, and there is a certainty of success.

Some people, to relieve themselves from the weight of excessive poor rates, would send our surplus population anywhere, if they could get rid of them. But it surely ought to be an important item in our consideration of this subject, that, from fellow feeling, we should not send people to a place where they would not do well. Surely we ought to rather seek the best place with most probabilities for their being comfortably prosperous and happy. There must be no selfish cruelty in getting rid of our superabundant population. It is not sufficient merely to pay for shipping them off and landing them abroad. You must select the best place for them, and organize means so that they shall be able to support themselves when they are living there. No one who knows the present state of our colonies would wish his brother to go there with the mistaken expectation of realizing a competency, either by mere labour or by trading; and no one ought to be so wanting in feeling

as to wish him to be exposed to the hardships he is certain
to encounter in the mere attempt. As regards ourselves,
such should be our disposition, before we think of sending
our poorer brethren to face what never can be imagined by
those that have never experienced it.

What then are we to do?

Send them where they will be sure to prosper (as I
said before), to the finest climate in the world—where
much clothing is unnecessary, where handsome wages can
be had, besides maintenance in addition; where a man
who abstains from intoxicating drink becomes provided for
for life, with his family, in two or three years' time; where
sickness hardly ever exists, and many English complaints
rapidly disappear—a land where labour, in connection with
outgoings and the cost of living, is tenfold more remunerative than in any English colony—a land where shivering
fogs and frosts are unknown, and where you can enjoy life
in a perpetual sunshine. It is a land where sheep are
1s. 8d. a-piece, fat bullocks, £2 a-piece; excellent horses,
£2 and £3 each; peon's wages, in hard cash, £38 per
annum—and where English female servants get £50 per
annum wages.

If our Government is not actuated by a proper feeling
in this respect; or, if there are State reasons from which
it is unable to sanction emigration to *foreign countries,*
why then let the rate-payers join together, and put their
hands into their own pockets, and tax themselves to form
an emigration fund, to rid themselves of the incubus of
the increasing poor rate that is weighing them down to the
ground; and let them charter ships at the cheapest possible

rate, to carry into comfort and prosperity those whom they cannot avoid supporting at home.

It must surely be a satisfactory reflection that not only are we relieving ourselves of the cost of supporting a redundant population, but that we are also effecting the certain happiness and maintenance of our destitute poor.

I have myself enjoyed this satisfaction, in having sent four large families from want in England to plenty abroad, who, when they had proved the place, sent me word "That they were all doing well, and should never be sufficiently thankful for my sending them there." "Tell brother David," said one of them, "that we have a better house over our heads than he has,"—this was one year after they had left England—"and that we are eating beef-steaks for breakfast."

With some people, seeing is believing. I can vouch for it in both of these ways, that, as regards a splendid country, for which, doubtless, a great future is in store, not one of our colonies can compare with South America.

Gentlemen, monied men, whom I have met, and who have come from Australia, New Zealand, the Cape of Good Hope, Natal, Canada, and California, have journeyed here, to see if the land and the prospects were better than where they came from. They all say that it is impossible to succeed where they have been; and the data that they have given me, as to the price of land, the capabilities of supporting stock, the wages, and the return for their investment, all show me that such will bear no comparison with the land of which I am speaking; and it is their determination to realize, where they are, whatever they can, out of the wreck of their estates, and transport themselves to where they can better succeed.

Notwithstanding what I have mentioned of these gentlemen, the undoubted fact exists that, superior as is this country that I have spoken of to all other places, it does not offer, at the present time, inducements or prospects to a capitalist to go there to farm *sheep*. How much less, then, are there inducements to go elsewhere. But it is solely to the man who is destitute, or who has only his labour to look to, and, perhaps, who is able only to do *slight* labour, that this is a land of plenty and comfort, and a certain place for the welfare and happiness of himself and his family.

Therefore, I pronounce that, while South America offers no prospect whatever to those wishing to invest in sheep, it presents the best possible emigration field for the industrious labouring man.

While one class of occupation, which with some is their sole one, seems now to cease to prosper, from the force of circumstances that none can at present control, still there is a good Providence resting over this fine country, disclosing glimpses to us of future prosperity. I will, therefore, here copy a statement made of what is stated to be authentic information, as to the *general* inducements offered to our countrymen of England, Ireland, and Scotland, to settle permanently in these regions :—

I. That the climate is healthy and favourable to long life, as in England or any other country of Europe.

II. That the cultivable lands are of unlimited extent, and require no outlay for clearing.

III. That it contains already, and especially in Buenos Ayres, the capital, a large and prosperous European population, composed of Italians, French, English, Scotch, Irish, Germans, and Portuguese.

IV. That the Government is perfectly liberal, its chief object being to preserve peace and promote the development of industry and commerce.

V. That, while the State religion is Roman Catholic, complete toleration is upheld, churches of all denominations being established at Buenos Ayres and other places where there are many English and German settlers.

VI. That there is a postal communication with England and the Continent, by powerful mail steamers, from Southampton, Liverpool, and Bordeaux.

VII. That the commercial policy of these countries is in the direction of free trade.

VIII. That, by a treaty between Great Britain and these Republics, foreigners are exempted from forced military service.

IX. That there is a sufficient number of British subjects in the Republic to render a knowledge of the Spanish language non-essential for emigrants, and that this language is capable of being acquired during a short residence more easily than any other tongue. Likewise, that an English newspaper is regularly published at Buenos Ayres, and also at the city and port of Rosario, and that there is an influential English bank and other institutions.

X. That English railway companies are opening up the country in all directions. One of their lines—the Rosario and Cordova Railway—will be 247 miles in length, and will, doubtless, ultimately cross the entire country to Chili, thus forming a highway for traffic between the Atlantic and Pacific.

XI. That the staple productions of the country are such as will at all times command the markets of the world, the principal exports being tallow, hides, and wool. While every effort is now being made to establish a scientific process of curing meat, which, at its present low price there and high price here, will enhance the produce of the country enormously.

XII. That the national debt of these countries is comparatively small, and is being gradually extinguished; that there are no direct taxes; and that the commerce of the country is increasing with great rapidity year after year. Our exports to the Argentine Republic amounted to £1,950,000 in 1865, and £2,844,000 in 1866.

XIII. That the acquisition of land is easy, and its tenure secure, and that additional and peculiar facilities for settlement of emigrants are now presented, from the circumstance that about one million of acres, on the sides of their line has been ceded to the Rosario and Cordova, or

I

Central Argentine, Railway Company (whose office is at 60, Gracechurch Street, London); and that a grant of 10,400 square miles in the fertile province of Cordova has been made to a gentleman who is about to transfer it to a London Company.

The only great want of this magnificent country is that of inhabitants. The position of many large fertile provinces is that of a rich unoccupied wilderness,—not sandy, barren, or rocky, like so many parts of inland Australia,—but everywhere heavy pasture on a deep and rich soil. Every one, therefore, who reads this, will easily understand the earnestness with which the surplus population of Europe may fairly and truthfully be invited to settle in these glorious regions which, under Providence, only want inhabitants to become the most happy and prosperous on the face of the earth.

The stream of emigration has, fortunately, of late years been directed, more than ever before, towards the River Plate, and it is increasing every year. The Argentine Republic, that was for so long, in common with the other countries of South America, an unknown land to the masses of our population, and is so still to many, has come to be better known, sought after, and appreciated. Accustomed as those are who wish to go abroad, to think only of New Zealand and New South Wales, at a distance of 16,000 miles, and a long arduous sea passage of 90—100 days' sail, they are agreeably surprised to find that there is a far superior and cheaper country much nearer our shores (being, in fact, about one-third less distant from us than the above places), that claims their attention and preference. More recent returns show that our British artizans, farmers, and labourers are beginning to emigrate in large numbers to the River Plate in preference either to the United States or to Australia; and there can be no question as to the wisdom of their choice.

On landing, they are attentively received by the Commission of Emigration, whose head-quarters are at Buenos Ayres and Rosario. The first assistance the Commission renders emigrants is to provide them with boats, to carry them ashore. If their means are small, they can apply to the Emigrants' Home, and there obtain free board and lodging until they procure suitable occupation, which is never long. This usually happens in a day or so, and often the services of emigrants are retained immediately they leave the vessel in which they have arrived from Europe. Comparatively few, however, have occasion to avail themselves of this useful asylum.

The following will prove the very high remuneration for services that is now given for the necessary and every-day requirements of labour:—

Per Annum.

Peons, that is shepherds and labourers of
every class, and men cooks   -   - £37 to £38
besides board and small house to live in rent free, or lodgings.

Female domestic servants   -   -   - £40 to £50
besides board and lodging.

Masons and carpenters, at per day -   10s. 6d. to 12s. 6d.
besides board and lodging.

Handy craftsmen, such as shoemakers, tailors, and capitas or managers, smiths, wheelwrights, &c., will earn even more than this. Washerwomen, sempstresses, and children, from ten to fifteen years of age, will earn in proportion. And these high wages are not likely to decrease for it is impossible to say how long a time, as the great want here *is people* in these unbounded lands. And when we remember that all their wages in hard cash is clear gain, as they are maintained free of cost, and can be invested at seven per cent. in the British Bank, a certain independence must be ensured in a short time.

To show the progress that these countries are making, we must turn to the statistics of the commercial returns. If we look at the returns of the year 1856 compared with 1865, we shall see what an excellent market England is securing for itself in this country. In 1856, British textile goods imported there were valued at a little over £250,000 or 218 per cent. less than what was sent there in 1865. While the total amount of all British imports to this country did not exceed in 1856 436,000, or 276 per cent. less than what was imported in 1865. The same increase we also observe with respect to the exports and imports from all other countries to South America.

The goods imported to Buenos Ayres
    were a total respectively, in 1864   - £4,370,134 0 0
In 1865 -   -   -   -   -   - 5,420,603 0 0

or an increase of twenty-four per cent. in 1865 over 1864.

The total exports, which show the development of the country as to its internal resources, sent to various market

of the world, show, for the year 1865, £4,399,355—about
four and a third million pounds sterling—of which about
two and a third were from wool alone. This article, wool,
stands at the head, as being by far the most considerable
and valuable article of export. Of this great amount of
four and a third million sterling pounds, one million and
fifty-two thousand worth were sent to Antwerp alone, for
consumption in the Northern Countries of Europe, Antwerp
being the channel for receiving them.

The great advance of wool production in these Republics
is one of the most positive signs of their material and
industrial progress. The following table, showing the
number of flocks of sheep, number of sheep, pounds
weight of wool, and sheep skins, from the year 1852,
demonstrate this most clearly:—

From Nov. 1st to Oct. 31st.			Flocks.	Sheep.	Million lbs. of Wool.	Bales, of 200 Skins each.
1852—3	...	...	3064	4,597,000	16	279,600
1853—4	...	...	3352	5,028,000	17	32,200
1854—5	...	...	3848	5,772,000	20	413,800
1855—6	...	...	4871	7,307,000	26	1,193,200
1856—7	...	...	5606	8,409,000	30	1,601,800
1857—8	...	...	5861	8,792,000	31	1,555,200
1858—9	...	...	7278	10,919,000	38	1,892,400
1859—60	...	...	6313	9,469,000	33	2,143,000
1860—1	...	...	9069	13,604,000	48	1,777,600
1861—2	...	...	10,104	15,044,000	53	2,153,200
1862—3	...	...	13,104	19,656,000	70	2,792,000
1863—4	...	...	14,438	21,656,000	77	3,346,600
1864—5	...	...	19,541	29,312,000	104	3,971,000
1865—6	...	...	22,467	33,701,000	120	4,152,200

I have in the above list omitted the units and hundreds in the number of sheep, and hundreds of thousands and under in the pounds weight of wool, as it is less confusing to see only gross amounts. The trade returns of British exports for the year 1864 is to the amount of £1,758,058, which stands higher in the list than Chili and Peru; and, as regards European countries, stands higher than Prussia, Sweden, Norway, Denmark, and many others with which we have trafficked for a much longer period. As regards also the debts of these countries, both foreign and internal, the interest of which is paid, unlike *North* America, with unfailing punctuality, they are comparatively small, and are gradually in course of being extinguished; the six per cent. bonds in the London market ranging from 90—100.

The official returns of nine years, ending in 1866, show the increase of emigrants into the Argentine Republic as regards the Port of Buenos Ayres alone.

	Arrived.	Applied to Asylum.
1858	4658	224
1859	4735	37
1860	5656	143
1861	6301	599
1862	6716	437
1863	10,408	545
1864	11,682	440
1865	11,767	1300
1866	13,959	—

The annexed table shows the nationality of the immigrants.

Nationality.	1862	1863	1864	1865	1866
Italians	3082	4494	5435	5001	6832
French	1561	2334	2736	2282	2333
Spanish	919	1377	1586	1701	1846
English	574	883	1015	1583	1310
Swiss	291	567	329	502	683
Germans	140	527	289	363	460
Belgians	50	100	100	100	182
Portuguese ...	25	50	50	50	70
North Americans ...	—	—	68	85	93
Others	74	76	73	100	150
Total	6716	10,408	11,682	11,767	13,959

Of these 66 per cent. were men, 16 per cent. women, and 18 per cent. children, making the 100. As to occupations, 70 per cent. were workmen, 20 per cent. artizans, and 10 per cent. without profession.

It will be seen by the above that the majority of immigrants were Italian. A similarity in the religion, language, and climate to that of their native country attracts them to the shores of the Argentine Republic. Their number in the province of Buenos Ayres alone is estimated at upwards of 70,000, of whom 40,000 reside in the City of Buenos Ayres. Their chief occupation is as boatmen and nursery gardeners, and as they lead very parsimonious lives, they amass considerable sums of money; and it is stated they remit annually to their friends in Europe as much as £100,000.

The number of Frenchmen in the country is estimated

at 25,000. Those from the Basque provinces are very considerable. The usual occupation of this class is in the saladeros or slaughtering houses. They also follow the trade of milkmen, which is entirely engrossed by them. Nearly all the barbers' shops in the city of Buenos Ayres are held by Frenchmen; whilst in the camps the retail store shops are generally kept by French Basques.

Spanish settlers are about 32,000, and have chiefly immigrated from the northern provinces of Spain. Germans and North Americans are comparatively few. But the British population, numbered at 32,000 in 1865, of whom 28,000 are Irish, reside for the most part in the country places, where they engage in rural pursuits and in tending sheep.

The thriving and prosperous condition of all these immigrants cannot more clearly be shown than by the amount of deposits vested in the English bank at Buenos Ayres. For each 100 depositors, 12¾ per cent. are Basques, 30½ Italians, 4¼ English, 8¾ French, 3¾ Germans, 12¼ Spanish, and 27½ various nationalities.

XI. How to Get to the River Plate.

Of late years the River Plate has been brought into rapid and frequent communication with this country, by means of steamers expressly constructed for the conveyance of produce and passengers. The facilities afforded will be best seen in the following list of lines at present in operation.

I. The Royal Mail Company's steamers sail monthly from Southampton to Rio Janeiro, which is connected with the River Plate by a branch line. Average length of voyage 33—35 days. Their office is in Moorgate Street.

II. The River Plate Association steamers sail between Liverpool, Monte Video, and Buenos Ayres. Their agents are at Liverpool.

III. The Liverpool, Brazil, and River Plate Company are dispatched twice every month. Messrs. Lamport and Holt, 21, Water Street, Liverpool, are the agents. These and the previous Company's steamers are not so fast as the first.

IV. The French Steam Company is the Messageries Impériales, whose vessels steam monthly from Bordeaux. Also,

V. The Genoa line from Marseilles.

I would add, by way of advice to the intending emigrant, that it is prudent, if you go by steam, to select vessels that are mail steamers, as their speed is much greater than the others, which are chiefly intended to convey produce and are not so much adapted for passenger traffic.

In addition to the above there are various lines of sailing vessels, well adapted to the use of immigrants, which start from Liverpool and Glasgow, besides Havre, Bordeaux, Marseilles, Bayonne, and Cadiz. The average length of voyage of these is 60—70 days, and the price of passage from £12—£16; the French and Spanish being £8 and £10.

The offices of any of these companies are easily found, and prices and other matters learnt on inquiry.

FINIS.

R. FOLKARD AND SON, PRINTERS, DEVONSHIRE STREET, QUEEN SQUARE.